W9-AYP-015

A View *from the*

BARN

Cal Bombay

Foreword by David Mainse

CROSSROADS CHRISTIAN COMMUNICATIONS INC.
1295 North Service Road,
Burlington, Ontario
L7R 4M2

ISBN 0-921702-81-7

Copyright 1997 **CAL R. BOMBAY**

Published by **CROSSROADS CHRISTIAN COMMUNICATIONS INC.**
1295 North Service Road, P.O. Box 5100, Burlington, Ontario, Canada L7R 4M2

All rights reserved. This publication may not be reproduced, stored in a retrieval system, or transmitted in whole or in part, in any form or by any means, without prior written permission of the publisher.

All Scripture quotations are from the New King James Version and are used with permission of Thomas Nelson Publishers. Copyright 1984.

CONTENTS

Chapter 7: Church? What's The Point?   131

Chapter 8: Fine-Feathered Friends   143

Chapter 9: Chickens, Goats, and One or Two Other Things   163

FOREWORD

Cal Bombay is my friend! I've known him since we were teenagers. We attended Bible college together and were members of the same class. After graduating, Cal and his wife, Mary, lived close to us. He was pastoring in Wellington, Ontario when I served in Brighton, Ontario.

Then Cal and Mary left for Africa. For the next 17 years we tried to keep in touch. During that time Cal founded a publishing house which became the largest such Christian effort in the entire continent, and we began the television ministry of Crossroads. In fact, Cal published our first Bible Study Correspondence Course for our viewers and shipped them to us from Africa.

*Then Cal, Mary, and their two children returned to Canada. Cal joined the Crossroads/**100 Huntley Street** team as our division head for Christian Missions Productions (CMP).*

He continues to make an outstanding contribution in many areas of ministry. Just recently he spent time in the south of Sudan where he helped negotiate the redemption of 319 slaves.

*Of course, Cal is beloved by millions for his popular TV commentaries. His wit, way with words and communication skills make him essential daily viewing. It amazes me how he can take a few hens, roosters, goats and a multitude of other farm experiences, apply them to life, and keep the attention of people everywhere. There are dozens I've come across who watch **100 Huntley Street** just for Cal's four to five minutes each day.*

Besides the daily TV commentaries, Cal is concentrating mainly on overseas missions and our Geoffrey R. Conway School of Broadcasting and Communications. For years he led our telephone ministry prayer lines. I know he'd be pleased if I encouraged you to call the Crossroads Regional Ministry Centres for prayer anytime — day or night. Someone who cares as deeply as Cal does for the Lord and for people will be available to pray with you:

- *Atlantic (902) 455-2600*
- *Prairies (403) 284-4721/944-0742*
- *Pacific (604) 430-1212*
- *Central (905) 335-0100 or (416) 929-1500*

David Mainse, President of Crossroads Christian Communications Inc.

INTRODUCTION

Over 1,150 commentaries later, my gardens, goats, chickens, barn, dogs, cats and other thinly-disguised friends, still provide food for thought. I simply cannot look at nature, and not see God and His handiwork.

This collection of commentaries, most of which centre in or around the barn, will tickle your soul and your conscience, more than your ears, I hope.

As strange as it may seem, reading some of them months, or even years after I wrote them, have helped me and ministered to me! I found that odd, since I wrote them all. Then I realized, it was not what I had written that hit me between the eyes, but what I have quoted from the greatest book on earth: the BIBLE.

I have one purpose in putting these commentaries in book form: to get some fundamental Scriptural truths past the brain and into the heart of every reader, then from the heart into everyday living. Just like music, humour too, can carry a message. I trust you get it!

There is another, better book to read and I recommend you read it cover to cover, over and over again. I speak of the Bible, of course.

I trust the truths I am trying to convey in this book will point you to the Word, both the Word in its written form, and the Word in living reality: Jesus Christ. May your love and devotion to Him and His lifestyle, be deeper and stronger because of what you read in these pages.

Please love Jesus enough to serve Him without reserve.

Cal R. Bombay

—

DEDICATION

To My Friend
My Companion
My Darling
My wife
Mary Elaine Bombay

Chapter 1

Food, Glorious Food!

YOU CAN'T ALWAYS TELL BY THE ENVELOPE!

An egg is an egg. Right? Some are big, some are small; some are white, some are brown; but unless an egg has been graded, you can never be quite sure what is in there until you crack it open. It's the same thing with letters. You can never be certain what's in a letter 'til you get past the envelope — and even more so with people. It's a dangerous thing to judge the contents before you get a glimpse on the inside. Let me illustrate.

The chicken coop is an interesting place these days. My new brown chickens have begun to really lay eggs. Their eggs are beautiful, with dark brown, strong shells. The old white hens are still holding up their own, but their shells are a little feeble, even though I supplement their diet with oyster shells to give them stronger envelopes.

Some are white and some are brown, but the shell is just a bit different; different envelopes, but the same contents.

I know, I know! Some people say that brown eggs are better eggs. Some say they even taste better. But according to the one scientific report I heard on the matter, the absolutely exclusive and single difference between a brown egg and a white egg is the colour — the envelope.

I was standing in our incoming mail department the other day. We get quite a few hundred pieces of mail every day. Some of it is called "white" mail. That means it has its own stamp on it, and it is not an envelope which we printed and sent out to our supporting partners. In fact, it may be blue, green, pink or brown, and we still call it "white" mail.

By looking at a piece of white mail, you can know nothing of its contents. It may be addressed to David, Lorna, Chuck or me. It may be addressed to Crossroads, *100 Huntley Street*, The Wheat Fund, or our Geoffrey R. Conway School of Broadcasting & Communications. But by looking at the envelope, you really have no idea what might be inside. It may be a donation to the ministry, or it may be a criticism about the number of times a day I feed our cats!

The same principle applies when looking at people, or eggs for that matter. By looking at an egg, you can be pretty sure what's inside: a yolk and the white of the egg. But even then, you can have some surprises. (I'm not even going to tell you what my daughter-in-law found inside an egg one time!) Yet, by looking at people, you cannot possibly know what is inside. Take Paul Bernardo, for instance. The envelope looked good. He was a clean-cut looking young fellow, but what was inside horrified Canada.

Just because the outside is white or brown, makes no difference. And with people, we are too quick to jump to conclusions because of the colour and size of the person. It's what's inside that counts. And what's inside, whether a person is pink or brown, beige or "bulgy," has little to do with what really is inside. Throughout the human race, the inside of most of us is just the same, although, occasionally there are some unwelcome surprises.

But what you *put on* can make a vast difference, not just in appearance, but in the quality of what is inside. Consider what Paul said when he wrote in Romans 13:14:

"But put on the Lord Jesus Christ, and make no provision for the flesh, to fulfil its lusts."

When you put on the Lord Jesus Christ, your other colourful attributes (or lack of colour, for that matter) are hidden with Christ in God. And when that is the case, the insides are affected too. Look at Ephesians 4:22-24:

"...that you put off, concerning your former conduct, the old man which grows corrupt according to the deceitful lusts, and be renewed in the spirit of your mind, and that you put on the new man which was created according to God, in true righteousness and holiness."

When God starts creating this new man, in true righteousness and holiness, you can know that God has gotten past the shell; the envelope; the colour.

There's little to be done with an egg, until at least it's cracked open. Then it can be fried, poached or scrambled. What's inside you can only be changed by God, and with your cooperation.

So, the next time you're tempted to jump to a conclusion about someone who appears different, be cool. Let God have a crack at him. He might just become your closest friend, especially if you are the one who shows real love.

APPRECIATION IS APPRECIATED

What do you do when someone throws a tomato at you? Duck? Well, I've been throwing tomatoes, gently, of course, at our staff here at *100 Huntley Street*. What they do with them is their own business, but what many do is simply catch them and make a tomato sandwich out of them. They all express their appreciation, some in different ways. You know what? I appreciate someone who appreciates what I do. Do you?

For some weeks now, I have been bringing in vegetables from my over-abundant supply. I always plant too many seeds into my gardens. It seems such a waste to have so much available garden space, and not use it. Sure, I have plenty of lawn, but that just produces work. Well, I guess it also produces something for the chickens and goats to eat when I throw the clippings into their runs. And, oh yes, it provides compost for my gardens which, of course, brings me right back to the subject of my gardens.

One of the many things I grow is tomatoes. Big, red, fleshy, sweet, beefsteak tomatoes. When ripened on the vine, there is no comparison to those hard tasteless "things" produced in winter under false pretences (false light and weather), although they're better than nothing!

So when the season is in full flourish with hot, sunny days, I can pick as much as a six-quart basket every day. But I've discovered I can't eat a full six-quart basket every day, not even with the help of my family. So, we freeze some, naturally, for use later in making spaghetti sauce. But I also give away a lot.

Anybody can have them. They don't even have to ask. I just bring them into the office and whoever I see first when I arrive in the morning gets some. After all, they deserve it for getting to work early!

But I've noticed, after a while, I become partial to some people. Not because others don't deserve or are entitled to some, but for another reason entirely.

The people who get my tomatoes, and whom I find myself seeking out in order to give them, caused me to suddenly realize something: these are the very ones who go out of their way to express their appreciation for these wonderful, tasty, delectable tomatoes. I appreciate being appreciated! For that reason, I find myself favouring those who express and show their appreciation.

In fact, some of the folk to whom I have given tomatoes, or something else from my gardens, have returned the favour by giving us a jar of homemade jam or some other nice stuff. And that's not even the reason I gave. I just gave because I had extra and wanted to give it away. But I do appreciate those who appreciate my tomatoes!

And just while I'm on this point, I want to express my appreciation to you who support this ministry. You can never really know how much we appreciate your support, your prayers, your... well... your tomatoes! And we try to show our appreciation by ministering to you and helping you in whatever ways we can.

I personally appreciate being appreciated. Are you the same? God is! Listen to this, in Deuteronomy 15:10:

"You shall surely give to Him, and your heart should not be grieved when you give to Him, because for this thing the Lord your God will bless you in all your works and in all to which you put your hand."

You can take it as a "given" that God appreciates and returns the favour when you favour Him or others with your gifts. Even in the matter of tithes (which are not even really gifts), they already belong to God. Yet God honours even that as we read in Malachi 3:10:

"'Bring all the tithes into the storehouse, that there may be food in My house, and try Me now in this,' says the Lord of hosts, 'If I will not open for you the windows of heaven and pour out for you such blessing that there will not be room enough to receive it.'"

I know I appreciate it when people help me in any little way. And I always want to somehow complete the cycle by doing something for them. It just seems the natural thing to do.

Now when it comes to tomatoes, I have an abundance and I give them away. I just hope no one decides to give them back, at full speed, from a strong, throwing arm! THAT kind of tomato I can do without! But, anything else you can throw our way. Well, don't feel restrained....

I'M REALLY INTO THE HARVEST!

Mary and I both have similar bad habits. I plant more seed in my gardens which produces more food than we can eat, and she puts more food on the table than any of us should reasonably eat. So we've developed another good habit out of this bad habit: we give it away! And that just makes it worse! People start giving stuff to us. Bruce, a friend of mine, puts it this way, "What goes around, comes around." Hidden behind this truth is a promise of God.

I can hardly believe the plenty that I have in my gardens these years. I have three rather large gardens. They are all about 25 feet by about 40 feet in size. From the earliest products, such as radishes that are ready shortly after spring, right through to those wonderful green vegetables that even fight off the frost in the late fall, we have plenty, with enough to give away.

I have been bringing in tomatoes and other things for the staff at *100 Huntley Street*. Everyone loves my big beefsteak tomatoes. I supply members of my family in Brantford, Kitchener and Cambridge. Even from the henhouse, eggs are plenty — certainly more than my doctor would be happy for me to eat all by myself.

But I suspect that some who get these benefits, don't realize the work and sweat that went into tilling the ground, the constant weeding late into the summer evenings, and the watering that is often needed. And, of course, there is the thinning and pruning and then, finally, the harvest. And I do that too. Now don't get me wrong. I really enjoy working the garden, and I gladly give away the extra, but it takes diligence. It also costs me the outflow of cash, not just for seeds, but for chicken feed as well. And let me assure you, feeding chickens is no chicken feed, if you'll pardon the pun. I've proven Proverbs 21:5 to be true:

"The plans of the diligent lead surely to plenty, but those of everyone who is hasty, surely to poverty."

Some folk wouldn't even think to plant a few seeds, even though it would save them quite a bit of cash. Yet some have learned to alleviate poverty with some effort. Look at Proverbs 28:19:

"He who tills his land will have plenty of bread, but he who follows frivolity will have poverty enough!"

Some people just fritter away time and opportunity. What could have been in hand (or in the pantry) is still just seed, sitting in a package, unused, and never grown.

But when people put a little effort, time and investment into their own future, they'll definitely have something to show for it. There is a basic law of seed time and harvest. And it's not just a law of nature. God Himself guarantees the extra; the plenty; the abundance! Look at what was reported when the people of God gave of their substance in Israel's history. It's found in 2 Chronicles 31:10:

"And Azariah the chief priest, from the house of Zadok, answered him and said, 'Since the people began to bring the offerings into the house of the Lord, we have had enough to eat and have plenty left, for the Lord has blessed His people; and what is left is this great abundance.'"

Did you notice the end of that verse? It says, *"...for the Lord has blessed His people; and what is left is this great abundance."* Some people get it into their heads that somehow or other the world or the government owes them a living. They sit under someone else's apple tree and hope that a few good apples will land in their lap. Rather than give, in both effort and substance, they want only to receive.

I dare say there are many who watch and benefit from *100 Huntley Street* on television and are even fed spiritually by it, but have seldom, if ever, raised a finger to help. Then they wonder why things are not going too well. Perhaps the answer is in Proverbs 3:9-10:

"Honour the Lord with your possessions, and with the firstfruits of all your increase so your barns will be filled with plenty, and your vats will overflow with new wine."

When we put a bit of blood, sweat and tears into the harvest, the law of seed time and harvest kicks in. Instead of waiting for something to fall into your lap, you'll be able, more and more, to help others.

Don't knock it if you haven't tried it. It works for me, both in my garden and in my giving!

THEY MUST HAVE BEEN LISTENING!

I just about got rid of them, but they began to do their duty again. So, once again, they've become profitable to me. That guarantees they're still safe, and I'll still feed them and water them. I'm talking about my old white hens. Suddenly they've picked up in their egg laying. That saved their lives. You don't suppose they were listening when I was telling someone their probable fate do you? Here's something you might care to ponder....

I have only 19 white Leghorn laying hens left in the barn. Some have gone the way of all flesh; others have entered the ministry. And when I say ministry, I mean not just me but my whole family.

I also have three silver-laced Wyandotte chickens left out there. Now these Wyandottes lay brown eggs, but at the moment I'm getting no brown eggs at all. Who knows, they may be on strike!

Now the white Leghorns are laying, but only very few every day. From 19 Leghorns I should get more than eight eggs a day.

I also have 25 new hens, just five months old, and they will begin laying eggs (brown ones) within about a month or so.

The other day, I was showing some people through my barn at their request. I was explaining that these new hens were going to be laying soon and that the old white Leghorns would be terminated as soon the others got well on the way. They must have been listening!

The next day I got fourteen white eggs, and that hasn't happened for months and months. They must have been listening and heard what their fate would be, based solely on their production. I don't dislike them, but I've got to have eggs and they've got to produce! If they don't, off come their heads! I'm not being mean. That's just the way it is on a farm. You can't afford to support an unfruitful hen. They become real liabilities.

I hope you're listening as well as my hens did! Listen to what Jesus said about the branches that don't produce what they should. They are a liability and, as a result, dispensable. It's found in John 15:2-3:

"Every branch in Me that does not bear fruit He takes away; and every branch that bears fruit He prunes, that it may bear more fruit. I am the vine, you are the branches. He who abides in Me, and I in him, bears much fruit; for without Me you can do nothing."

Some may say, "I have faith and I pray. After all, I am a child of God." Well, good for you. But Jesus talks about faith and duty in Luke 17:7-10. Just because you have faith doesn't insulate you from duty. Listen:

"And which of you, having a servant ploughing or tending sheep, will say to him when he has come in from the field, 'Come at once and sit down to eat'? But will he not rather say to him, 'Prepare something for my supper, and gird yourself and serve me till I have eaten and drunk, and afterward you will eat and drink'? Does he thank that servant because he did the things that were commanded him? I think not. So likewise you, when you have done all those things which you are commanded, say, 'We are unprofitable servants. 'We have done what was our duty to do.'"

But hold on a minute. Does that mean I'm cast off forever? I think not.

The Apostle Paul and a fellow by the name of Philemon had both found one young man, Onesimus by name, totally useless. But Paul must have talked to him a bit, and he must have listened (like my chickens). Let's read what Paul wrote about this young man in Philemon 1:10-11:

"I appeal to you for my son Onesimus, whom I have begotten while in my chains, who once was unprofitable to you, but now is profitable to you and to me."

I guess my question to you is: Are you listening? Do you hear what God is saying about unprofitable servants, unfruitful branches?

Just like Onesimus became dutiful again, you can listen and change your ways, and increase your profitability to God. You can be bearing fruit again for God. And God will not cut you off.

I'm probably going to keep the old white hens, now that they're producing again!

Are you listening? Are you doing your duty?

REACHING FOR THE SKY

Weeds aside, a garden is a wonderful thing to watch as it grows. Different plants grow in different forms, and have different fruit. Some grow straight up, and others grow across the ground. But one thing they all have in common: they all reach for the sky, with either stocks or leaves, or both. It's the sun that they're always reaching for. Pity the poor fruitless plant that's stuck in the shadows.

It's a fascinating thing to watch things grow. When they first come out of the earth, they grow straight up — reaching for the sun. Even such things as pumpkins, squash and cucumbers come straight up at first, always reaching for the sun. I have climbing beans, which send out their little fine tentacles and grab at anything that is up. Then they take a firm grip and continue growing upward toward the sun. I provide the string, hanging from a narrow board for the beans to climb. I like to encourage them to grow toward the sun.

Even the leaves of the heavy pumpkin vines, when they finally ease over to spread across the soil, always grow up toward the sun.

One of the amazing things is that as the sun moves across the sky, some of them slowly turn in order to take full advantage of the sun.

Some parts of my gardens are in the shadow of the barn part of the day and, at one edge, under the shadows of some nearby trees in the early evening. They don't do as well as those which get all of the sun that's available. Their growth is impeded. Even though they get the same amount of rain as the others, they are not as large and lush as those that get both sun and rain.

When new life starts, it is all equal opportunity. For the first few days (and even weeks), they grow at the same rate, and are just as large in the shadows as the plants which get more sun. But it's not too long before you see an increasing difference in the plants which get more sun, and those that have to contend with shadows and less direct sunlight.

I think Christian people are much the same. The new birth — coming to life and faith in Jesus Christ — is equal for all. But some remain in the shadows. And that's where our new life in Christ differs from the life of a plant. Plants have no opportunity to uproot themselves and walk over into a place where there's more light.

As Christians, we do! We don't have to stay in the shadows. We can take deliberate action and walk from the shadows into the Light. And, as Christians, Jesus is our Light. Listen to 1 John 1:7:

"But if we walk in the light as He is in the light, we have fellowship

with one another, and the blood of Jesus Christ His Son cleanses us from all sin."

So we need to walk in the light, always reaching upward toward the Son of God, Jesus, who is the Author of Life; the One who brings us to full growth. The Apostle Paul urges us to get away from the shadows — staying away from the dark things of life — because plants that grow in the shadows don't bear much fruit at all. Listen to Ephesians 5:11:

"And have no fellowship with the unfruitful works of darkness, but rather expose them."

Get out into the light. Leave the unfruitful shadows which inhibit your growth and your spiritual health. Run from them. Get your life into the full benefit of life in the Son, who Himself said in John 15:4:

"Abide in Me, and I in you. As the branch cannot bear fruit of itself, unless it abides in the vine, neither can you, unless you abide in Me."

We are the planting of God, and just as I have expectations from my garden, so God has expectations from us. A few verses later in the same chapter, Jesus said in verse 16:

"You did not choose Me, but I chose you and appointed you that you should go and bear fruit, and that your fruit should remain, that whatever you ask the Father in My name He may give you."

If you want to get things done for God, and if you want to bear fruit that remains, you've got to come out of the darkness (or out of the shadows) and start reaching for the sky. Start reaching for the Son; the Son of God!

YOU CAN ALWAYS PLANT AGAIN!

My first planting of corn ran into trouble: at first, too much rain and then, too much hot dry weather. But so what? I had more seed, so I planted it again. This time it took root. If a farmer gave up when his first planting failed, where do you suppose we'd get the harvest? Seeds don't plant themselves! And you can always plant again! Don't be too quick to give up!

Spring is usually the time for planting; for giving the house a good cleaning; for falling in love. It's usually the time when life takes on a fresh and new dimension in many ways. But spring doesn't always turn out the way you would expect, or hope.

Recently, I saw a couple sitting on a park bench, making cow's eyes at each other. They didn't seem to be saying a word, just looking into each other's eyes. Something seemed to be coming to life. Well... almost! The young fellow said something, and the cow's eyes turned to cold eyes as the young gal stood and walked away. Something almost came to life.

It's like cleaning the house. Everything is polished and clean and sparkling after the spring cleaning. It's almost like the house takes on a new life. Then someone comes in with dirty feet, or a dust storm blows through, and the one who put in all the hard work slowly lets their shoulders droop. Well, it was clean for a while!

It's the same sometimes at planting time. I recall how, late one spring evening, I rushed some corn, beans and peas into the garden. They were planted in perfect rows and perfect planting depth. To top it off, rain was predicted the same night. Well, the rain came — and in drenching sheets it came! It soaked the garden in inches of water that stayed for days, and that was followed by a solid nine days of bone dry heat. The seeds never came up, even though they may have germinated. They never got to the surface of the soil because the clay soil was baked as solid as brick by the sun. The little bit of life that might have started was dead before it got to the light of day.

Well, it's not the first time I planted seeds that either rotted or were killed in some other way. But I found out something very important a few years ago: *You can always plant again*. You can stir up the soil, plant the seeds again and hope for the best. So I did! I planted seeds again and this time I hoped and prayed. Soon the beans, corn, beets and Swiss chard grew well and the harvest was plentiful.

The philosophy behind farming is that *you never give up.* Just because one planting doesn't take, it doesn't mean that you are defeated forever. You can always plant again.

But one setback, one defeat, and sometimes even an *imagined* defeat, puts some people right out of action. Even the thought of putting in a second planting is too "unguaranteed" for some people. One failure, one scare, and they're done. It's a bit like what Solomon said in Proverbs 22:13:

"The lazy man says, 'There is a lion outside! I shall be slain in the streets!'"

Some may say, "Don't ask me to expose myself again. I might fail!" And unfortunately, because the one person in whom they planted the seeds of the Gospel refused and rejected that seed, they're just going to back off. Listen to what David says in Psalms 126:6:

"He who continually goes forth weeping, bearing seed for sowing, shall doubtless come again with rejoicing, bringing his sheaves with him."

Sowing the seed is our responsibility. Whether or not it grows, is not. And just because the first planting doesn't "take," doesn't mean that we should give up. God knows when and how to make it germinate in the hearts of those who hear the Gospel. Never give up! Listen to Mark 4:26-28:

"And He [Jesus] said, 'The kingdom of God is as if a man should scatter seed on the ground, and should sleep by night and rise by day, and the seed should sprout and grow, he himself does not know how. For the earth yields crops by itself: first the blade, then the head, after that the full grain in the head.'"

When you tell someone of God's love in sending Jesus Christ to literally "save" them and they don't respond immediately, don't worry, just keep planting seed. Eventually the harvest will come. God will see to that!

UNUSED SEEDS ROT IF NOT USED

I have some unused seeds which were left in their partly-used packages. But they got damp and rather than grow, they've sprouted and immediately died and rotted because they had no soil. Seeds have to be planted if we expect them to grow fruit. They have to literally go into the soil and die, before they can be useful. Do you have some unplanted seeds in danger of rotting? *"Most assuredly, I say to you, unless a grain of wheat falls into the ground and dies, it remains alone; but if it dies, it produces much grain."* Jesus said that in John 12:24!

In my little greenhouse, I have all kinds of plants growing. There are two varieties of pumpkins I've started. I also have cabbage, cauliflower, brussels sprouts, pepper squash, okra, watermelon, and even rhubarb. Eggplant is something new this year and, of course, green peppers. There are flowers of all kinds: foxglove, marigold, pampas grass, pansies, and a lot more.

But rather than plant the whole package of seeds, in some cases, I left some in packages. These hang over the trays of planted seed. What I did not realize was that seeds in a package, when wet, will simply rot. They are not fruitful because they have no soil — nothing to feed on. For seeds to grow, they have to be put in good soil.

Unfortunately, I have a lot of unplanted seeds which got wet, but never got life. I saved some of those seeds — I guess a little like a savings account — for future use. But when stored in the wrong place, they not only don't bear fruit, they rot.

Do you remember what Jesus said when He was talking about sowing seed in rocky soil, shallow soil and good soil? Listen to Luke 8:11:

"Now the parable is this: The seed is the Word of God."

I am occasionally dismayed when I preach the Word of God in a church, and there seem to be no visible results. One of our telephone prayer partners reminded me that seed takes time to grow. However, the seed has been sown. I was reminded that I had done my part. Someone under God's hand will water that seed. Then God will be the one who germinates the life, as a result of the Word, in the hearts of people. Look at 1 Corinthians 3:7:

"So then neither he who plants is anything, nor he who waters, but God who gives the increase."

I am only responsible for what God calls me to do. He is the One who makes the seed take root and grow and produce fruit. But the devil does his crooked best to keep the seed from bearing fruit. Look at Matthew 13:19-20:

"When anyone hears the Word of the kingdom, and does not understand it, then the wicked one comes and snatches away what was sown in his heart. This is he who received seed by the wayside. But he who received seed on the good ground is he who hears the Word and understands it, who indeed bears fruit and produces: some a hundredfold, some sixty, some thirty."

But what bothers me is that there is so much seed that is simply not being sown. It sits in our savings accounts and rots. What good is a rotten treasure? If you're not going to plant it, for goodness sake, don't put it up on a shelf where it can rust, rot or be stolen. Hear what Jesus said in Matthew 6:20:

"But lay up for yourselves treasures in heaven, where neither moth nor rust destroys and where thieves do not break in and steal."

Canada is one of the richest nations in the world. We have so much that a lot of it is simply rotting in packages. It has to be planted. There's a lot of good soil, receptive soil, ready soil in this great land of ours and around the world. Hearts are ready and open to the truth of God's Word, but we've got to plant it. Missions is the call of the whole Church.

In a letter I wrote to our partners in perhaps a funny, yet serious way, I asked you to plant some seeds in this nation through *100 Huntley Street*. Many people responded and, as a result, much seed was sown.

Asking for financial support is not the most loved job any of us have at the Crossroads Centre. Yet if we didn't ask, we wouldn't receive and, therefore, seed would not be sown.

We are not into gimmicks. We just trust that people will give, both to *100 Huntley Street* and to their local church, because they love souls.

So much unused seed!

MATURITY COMES - BE PATIENT

Watermelons are one of my favourite summer refreshments. When I buy them, I can generally count on them being ripe and ready; mature and juicy. When I grow them myself, I have a real problem knowing when they are ready to eat. I've wasted quite a few because they both "looked" ready and "sounded" mature when I plunked them with my finger. Some people are a bit the same. They look and sound ready for leadership, but they're still just pink inside.

This past summer, I became somewhat impatient with my garden, partly through ignorance and partly because I just wanted to rush things along. First of all, I suppose I should explain my ignorance. It's hard to tell when a watermelon is really ready (at least it is for me). The year before, I had picked a watermelon because it "looked" ready. But when I got it into the house, cooled it off in the refrigerator and then cut it open with a big knife, it was hardly pink. In fact, it was almost white, with no sign of the mature, juicy, red I expected. So, I made some inquiries.

"How do you know when a watermelon is ripe?" I asked my knowledgeable sister. "You bang it with a finger, like this, and you can tell when it "sounds" right. It will sound sort of hollow," she explained.

So last year, I was out in my garden from early August, banging away with my fingers on my watermelons. Even though they "looked" ready, I wasn't sure whether they "sounded" ready! So I waited a bit longer. One day after a rain, I noticed one of the watermelons had split open. It was juicy red and obviously ready. So I washed, sliced and ate it. (They're miniature watermelons by the way, about the size of a cantaloupe.)

So, I looked at the rest that were planted at the same time. They all "looked" ready, and now it seemed they "sounded" ready too. So I picked a few with a mouth-watering plan in mind. I would surprise my family with cold watermelon for dessert after supper. Supper came and went, and I prepared to "wow" them with my watermelons. I went out to the refrigerator, pulled them out, and sliced the first one open. Light pink! Not ready. It "looked" mature and "sounded" ready. They were all light pink — unready; immature. I admit that sometimes I'm still ignorant when it comes to knowing when a watermelon is really ready.

Looks can be deceiving! So can sounds!

Christians come in varying degrees of maturity as well. They may look like mature Christians, and even may have mastered some of the pat phrases many Christians use, but they may not be very mature. Sometimes we expect too much from new Christians too soon. They're simply not ready. Certainly they are Christians and they are as "saved" as any other believer in Jesus Christ, but they simply haven't grown enough to be ready for use in the Church, or for responsibility in the Church. When the Apostle Paul wrote to Timothy about the appointment of Christian leaders, he said among other things in 2 Timothy 3:6:

"...not a novice, lest being puffed up with pride he fall into the same condemnation as the devil."

Maturity is needed in leadership. Paul also advised the Corinthians when it came to the matter of speaking in tongues and spiritual gifts. He said in 1 Corinthians 14:20:

"Brethren, do not be children in understanding; however, in malice be babes, but in understanding be mature."

The Apostle Peter also said something to the same effect in 2 Peter 3:16-18:

"...some things [are] hard to understand, which untaught and unstable people twist to their own destruction, as they do also the rest of the Scriptures. You therefore, beloved, since you know this beforehand, beware lest you also fall from your own steadfastness, being led away with the error of the wicked; but grow in the grace and knowledge of our Lord and Saviour Jesus Christ. To Him be the glory both now and forever. Amen."

Just like you can't expect a watermelon to be ready before its time, so it is with young Christians. They may look and sound ready, but when the knife of life cuts to the core, we find immaturity and waste.

That's why there should always be enough time given for the maturing process and growth in the grace of our Lord Jesus Christ before we expect perfection on the part of new Christians.

The fact of the matter is this: When you were a child, you were a child! Me, too!

Therefore, remember that all new Christians start out as babes in Christ. Give them a chance!

HOW VALUABLE IS IT TO YOU?

What do you do when you have more tomatoes than you need right now? Well, after eating as much as is reasonable, you preserve as much as you can for the colder days ahead, right? Right! What do you do when your spiritual life is at a high, and Christian fellowship, God's Word, and His provisions are abundant? You take in and preserve as much as you can, because cold weather does come!

In August, tomatoes are for sale everywhere. Not only do the supermarkets offer tomatoes at the cheapest price ever, but along almost every country road there are little stands offering vegetables for sale. And tomatoes are always a part of that offering. Even in front of private homes in town, you can see little stands with their extra tomatoes for sale. Tomatoes are everywhere in abundance and as cheap as you'll ever get them.

I had a tomato once, bigger than I had ever grown before. It weighed 1,563 grams. That's about three and a half pounds. I've personally never seen a larger tomato. Yet that tomato, along with others in a six-quart basket, can be bought for about two dollars at current August prices. That's about thirty cents a pound. Let's face it folks, August is the month to buy tomatoes. Even in supermarkets they're down to sixty-nine cents a pound.

In fact, we're so surrounded by such abundance in August that we almost act like it will last forever. There are even some people who take advantage of the abundance but, because of procrastination, they'll find in a few weeks it will be too late. The availability will be down and the prices will be up. By February, we will have to pay about $1.99 a pound for hard and flavourless hothouse tomatoes.

August is the time for tomatoes. They are much more expensive in the winter months. When you're really hungry for a bit of tomato in a salad or in a side dish, you'll even be willing to pay the higher price for it.

And to think I usually throw slightly damaged tomatoes to the chickens! In August, we don't value them very highly. It's when the winter months come that we begin to value them. It's when there's an abundance that it's time to freeze, eat and preserve as much as we can. Then winter comes....

There's a parallel here with our spiritual experience. When we are in the thick of Christian peace and tranquility, and life is going along well — when the climate of faith around us is warm and everything is sweetness and joy — there is a tendency to disregard and undervalue our personal relationship with the Lord. When things go well, we somehow don't think we need God quite as much.

But then winter comes. We have trials and perhaps are cut off from Christian fellowship for some reason. That's when our faith becomes much more precious to us. That's when we wish we had laid up a bit more in store and spent more time in the Word, taking advantage of the abundance. Listen to what the apostle says in 1 Peter 1:6-7:

"In this you greatly rejoice, though now for a little while, if need be, you have been grieved by various trials, that the genuineness of your faith, being much more precious than gold that perishes, though it is tested by fire, may be found to praise, honour, and glory at the revelation of Jesus Christ."

When adversity comes, the depth of the value you place on your faith in the good times will keep you strong through the fire.

As a Christian, I urge you to take your faith in Jesus Christ with deep seriousness. Preserve and store up your knowledge and relationship with God. For just as surely as the season of fresh garden tomatoes will pass, so will the ease and plenty of life pass into another season.

You who have found a wonderful relationship with God, know how very precious and valued Jesus becomes. But as years go by, there is a tendency to take Him and His provisions for granted. We almost treat our faith as trite or commonplace. This in no way devalues the Lord, but it does betray our attitude toward the things of God. May we always be able to say with the apostle in 1 Peter 2:7:

"Therefore, to you who believe, He is precious...."

How valuable is the Lord to you?

INVASION

I like raspberries. Four years ago, I had no raspberries. This year, I almost feel threatened by the growth and spread of my raspberry patch. It's my own fault, of course. I put them there in the first place. But when you start a raspberry patch, you'd better be certain that you have both the time and the know-how to control them. And I've never met anyone yet who would want their lives controlled by a raspberry.

Friends of *100 Huntley Street* who live just down the highway from us, one day telephoned us. They had a very kind offer. They had some ever-bearing raspberries which had begun to grow in a much larger patch than they anticipated. Rather than just dig them out, they offered them to us for our garden.

Well, since I had plenty of room for them and since they are several dollars a pint now (and I love fresh raspberries), I agreed quickly. I drove over to their house to dig them so I could plant my new berry patch. I think it was in June or July of 1992. To my utter surprise, I received a small crop that same August through October.

I planted those twenty canes in one straight row. Only one died. All the rest in my nice neat row, bore big luscious, sweet, red raspberries.

The next year, to my delight, the row thickened. And from August through to October we had fresh raspberries often. Raspberries are so good! Then in 1994, so many new plants came up and the row became so wide and thick that it was difficult to pick them all.

Now you must realize that during this whole process, I was learning a few things about raspberries. Since I hadn't learned it all, I decided to simply cut a path down through the middle of this now very wide row, and divide it into two rows. I thought I was pretty smart! I wasn't. This year they came up thicker and taller, in a row fully five or six feet wide. They are taking over! Their roots shoot out underground, and come up wherever there is space. If I'm not careful, they'll soon take over the garden.

I almost feel like I should sit on the back porch of the house at night with a gun to guard myself against their encroachments. (Actually, I've read a book about them and I know what to do this fall and winter.)

As much as I like raspberries, I can't allow them to crowd out everything else in my garden. You can survive on raspberries I suppose, but I love the variety of food in my garden. I've found things in my life that are like raspberries. They're quite legitimate and I like them, but there's more to a healthy, balanced life than just raspberries.

I'm not alone in my kind of situation. Yet we cannot allow our whole lives to be taken over by the one thing we like more than everything else, as good as it may be. It may one day become detestable to us.

I like the key verse of Circle Square Ranch. It reflects balance in life, in interests and in activity. Look at Luke 2:52:

"And Jesus increased in wisdom and stature, and in favour with God and men."

But some people's favourite raspberry in their garden of life, is a doctrinal emphasis. They want to always be involved with healing, deliverance, discipleship, eschatology, or even just doctrine itself. These things are good and legitimate, but they must be kept in balance, otherwise it can take over your whole life. It is possible to have too much of a good thing. Paul's instructions to young Timothy called for a well-rounded ministry. Look at 2 Timothy 4:2-4:

"Preach the Word! Be ready in season and out of season. Convince, rebuke, exhort, with all longsuffering and teaching. For the time will come when they will not endure sound doctrine, but according to their own desires, because they have itching ears, they will heap up for themselves teachers; and they will turn their ears away from the truth, and be turned aside to fables."

If I turn a deaf ear to the warnings that raspberries are taking over my garden, I've as good as lost it.

If there is something in your life (good and legitimate as it is) that is beginning to take up too much of you, be warned. Yes, you can probably keep it, but KEEP IT UNDER CONTROL! Keep your life in balance!

WHEN THE DEAD FALLS OFF

Well, I found out the secret! Now I know for certain when a watermelon is ripe. This summer, I'm not going to waste a lot of good watermelons by trying to pick them too soon. No more wasting months of growth by pulling them off the vine too soon. Now I know! How many new young watermelons I've wasted, and how many new young Christians have been hurt badly before they were ready.

Some time ago when Babbie Mason was singing on *100 Huntley Street*, I did a commentary about ripening watermelons. I admitted my ignorance on how to know when a watermelon is actually ripe. Well, Babbie's husband Charles was with her, sitting in the audience. When I finished my commentary, he called me over with a big grin on his face and said, "I can tell you how to know when a watermelon is ripe. I come from a farming background, and my daddy told me how to know."

Well, I'm always interested in my "continuing education," so I listened. Charles said, "Right at the stem where the watermelon grows on the vine, there is a little leaf; just a small leaf." He indicated with his fingers, about an inch long. He continued by saying, "When that little leaf dries up and turns brown or falls off, your watermelon is ripe."

I asked, "That's all there is to it?" Charles affirmed that it was. I asked him how long it takes and he answered, "As long as it takes!"

Well, I knew right away that I had another commentary! Later we joked about him getting royalties on that line in my commentary. It was a moot point since I don't even get royalties myself!

You see, some new Christians take a bit more time maturing than others. It takes more time for the old things from the old life to fall away, and for the full bloom of Christian life to take hold. It is often a process when learning and growing in faith and obedience: time with other Christians, time studying God's Word and time on one's knees before God.

Some of us who have been Christians for some years expect new Christians to somehow be perfect immediately, as though we were perfect ourselves! When we see an old and evil habit that has yet to be broken, we become judgmental. But stop for a moment. We're ALL still under construction!

Yes, it's true that being born again, saved, or coming to faith in Christ (whichever term suits you) is instantaneous. But maturing and dropping off the sinful habits of a lifetime often takes time.

How long does it take? As long as it takes!

A growing Christian is under continual construction, just like the watermelon as it is growing and getting virtue and value in life. It's putting off the dead from the old unregenerate life. For example, look at Ephesians 4:21-23:

"...if indeed you have heard Him and have been taught by Him, as the truth is in Jesus: that you put off, concerning your former conduct, the old man which grows corrupt according to the deceitful lusts, and be renewed in the spirit of your mind."

Not only are there things from the past life which must be put off, but there are things that new Christians need time to put on. Some of these things are listed in Colossians 3:12-14:

"Therefore, as the elect of God, holy and beloved, put on tender mercies, kindness, humility, meekness, longsuffering; bearing with one another, and forgiving one another, if anyone has a complaint against another; even as Christ forgave you, so you also must do. But above all these things put on love, which is the bond of perfection."

You can be certain this summer when I start picking the watermelons for my table, they will be the ones whose last little leaf has died and fallen off. They will be ripe for my use.

Paul summarizes the Christian growth clearly in 2 Corinthians 5:17:

"Therefore, if anyone is in Christ, he is a new creation; old things have passed away; behold, all things have become new."

The key words here are "HAVE BECOME"!

Even the Apostle Paul had to take time to mature enough so that God could use him. His conversion to Christ was instantaneous, but the growing process started in the company of some disciples. Then he went into the desert with God for some years before his dead leaves fell off and his new life came into full fruition.

So, the next time you're tempted to come down hard on a new Christian, don't rip that little green leaf off. Let it die a natural death under the teaching of God's Word and Spirit. That's when the unripe white will become pink and, eventually, a full luscious red — ready for use in God's kingdom!

Chapter 2

Sowing Good Seed In Good Soil

YOU HAVE TO KNOW WHAT TO LOOK FOR

Someone from Kingston very kindly sent me a beautiful calendar illustrated with chickens. Whoever it was, thank you! But as I was going through the pictures, I noticed something inconsistent with what I happen to know as fact. One picture seems okay on the surface, but if you know anything much about chickens and eggs, you have to be a little suspicious. And it's not wrong to be cautious and suspicious in some things. Let me explain:

This beautiful calendar had every month illustrated by a full-colour photograph of various breeds of chickens. Some of them I don't recognize. Others I do, such as the Plymouth (barred) Rock which is good for both eggs and meat. I had one of these hens myself. Then there is the very common chicken, the white Leghorn. I have at least 20 of them. They are excellent egg layers, but pretty skimpy when it comes to meat.

Another one is the black Australorp hen. They are big chickens and make excellent roasts. They also lay eggs, of course. But then if they didn't, they wouldn't even exist, would they?

When I was looking through the calendar, I think I detected an inconsistency. It's in one of the pictures. The untrained eye might not even catch it. Now, I am assuming that the hen, which happens to be a Plymouth Rock, is setting on these eggs with the eventual aim of spending 21 days until they hatch. The caption under the picture says, "Two more nights and she'll have a dozen."

Maybe she's just settling down to simply lay another egg. But, the fact of the matter is, the Plymouth Rock hen can only lay brown eggs, and there are three white eggs there. So perhaps we have to change our assumption. Maybe she is just going to lay another egg where some white leghorns (which lay only white eggs) have already done their day's work.

The only way to be really sure is to be more familiar with this chicken coop and its inhabitants. The only other possibility is that the photographer simply placed a few extra eggs under her as props to enhance the beauty of the photograph. And the more I think about it, that's what I think has happened. Hens, whether they are setting or laying, have a tendency to totally cover all the eggs under them. So this is probably posed; a slight deception.

But to know this for certain, you must be familiar with the coop, and all its contents and inhabitants. Otherwise you could be easily deceived. The caption is deceptive. You can't believe everything you see, hear or read. Deception is all around us.

And the worst deception of all has nothing to do with chickens and eggs. It has to do with our relationship with God, our awareness of sin and our understanding of His Word.

As far as sin is concerned, the Bible says in 1 Corinthians 6:9-10:

"Do you not know that the unrighteous will not inherit the kingdom of God? Do not be deceived. Neither fornicators, nor idolaters, nor adulterers, nor homosexuals, nor sodomites, nor thieves, nor covetous, nor drunkards, nor revilers, nor extortioners will inherit the kingdom of God."

Then in Galatians 6:7 we read:

"Do not be deceived, God is not mocked; for whatever a man sows, that he will also reap."

And there just happens to be people in this wicked world of ours who, for personal advantage, teach and preach half truths, deceptions, and rationalizations of their personal wickedness. Look at what the Scriptures say about that in Colossians 2:8:

"Beware lest anyone cheat you through philosophy and empty deceit, according to the tradition of men, according to the basic principles of the world, and not according to Christ."

What I'm saying is that you cannot believe everything you hear, see and read. The Apostle Paul had some very harsh things to say to one such manipulator of truth. It's recorded in Acts 13:10. Listen to what Paul said:

"...O full of all deceit and all fraud, you son of the devil, you enemy of all righteousness, will you not cease perverting the straight ways of the Lord?"

Eggs and chickens posed for a pretty picture are one thing, but deceptions that touch your soul and your eternal salvation are deeply serious. That's why I urge you to familiarize yourself with the facts, and the Bible has all the facts. You don't have to be taken in by fraudulent preaching or teaching. Read it for yourself!

YOU HAVE TO CRACK IT OPEN TO REALLY KNOW

One day when I showed three eggs on television, I wondered what was inside each one. I thought I knew, but I couldn't be sure until I cracked them open. So, just to satisfy my curiosity (and possibly yours as well), I decided to crack them open to see what really was inside those three chicken eggs.

I had used those three eggs to illustrate a point about our giving as Christians. After the program, as I was having my lunch, several young people who had been in the studio audience asked me if the large one was a double-yolked egg. I said it probably was, but it might possibly even have three yolks at that size. Then they asked me what was in the little egg. I said I wasn't sure, but I doubted if there was even a yolk in such a small egg. On the other hand, the regular-sized egg would be quite predictable. One yolk! Not too much doubt about that egg!

So, I decided to crack them open and find out exactly what was in each egg. First, I cracked the regular-sized egg and as I expected: one yolk. Next, came the small egg and, sure enough, as I suspected: nothing but tasteless white. Next and last, came the "biggy"! Well, I thought it might have had three yolks, but it only had two. The point is this: You can never be sure until you crack an egg open!

This illustrates something very important to me. What kind of books do you crack open? There are a lot of trashy books out there in the market place and they do no good for you at all. They are like the little egg with no yolk: they leave an emptiness; a dribble of nothingness.

On the other hand, there are some very good books that are well worth reading because they have substance. They leave you with increased knowledge; a feeding of the intellect. You feel like you've read something worthwhile. That to me is like the regular-sized egg, with a healthy yolk inside. But you have to crack it open and devour it before it does you any good.

But that large egg, with more yolk than can be normally expected, to me illustrates the Book of all books: the Bible. This Book, in fact, has a total of 66 books in it. The good that can come from the Bible far exceeds what can be expected from any other book in the world.

This Book, like the double-yolked egg, will leave you with something well worth devouring which does you an immense amount of good. There's real food value in the Book of books!

Look at one of the secrets in this Book that you may otherwise never find, unless you crack it open. It's found in Romans 16:25-26:

"Now to Him who is able to establish you according to my Gospel and the preaching of Jesus Christ, according to the revelation of the mystery which was kept secret since the world began but now has been made manifest, and by the prophetic Scriptures has been made known to all nations, according to the commandment of the everlasting God, for obedience to the faith...."

And that mystery, which is no longer a mystery, is explained in 1 John 2:25:

"And this is the promise that He has promised us — eternal life."

So, crack the Book open and look into it! Search out its secrets. Solve the mystery of its hidden truths. Look at what Jesus said in John 5:39:

"You search the Scriptures, for in them you think you have eternal life; and these are they which testify of Me."

In looking into the Book, don't get so wrapped up in the theology, the history, the drama and the literary beauty that you miss the main point. Jesus said, *"...these are they which testify of ME"* (John 5:39). Jesus is like the yolk — the Real Value — the very Life of the Book.

One day, Jesus said when He was praying to God the Father (John 17:3):

"And this is eternal life, that they may know You, the only true God, and Jesus Christ whom You have sent."

Don't settle for anything less than the best. Certainly not the trashy books with no content. And don't be satisfied merely with classic and educational literature, as good as it is. Go for the best nourishment you can ever find: the Bible, the very Word of God.

MORE THAN ENOUGH

In a good season, I am almost overwhelmed with tomatoes. Big luscious, rich, meaty, tasty tomatoes. I've given bushels away. We've canned and frozen as much as we would need during the winter months. Those bountiful harvests bring great joy to my heart, not to mention, great satisfaction to my stomach! But none of it would have happened unless I had put a few seeds into the ground! Seed time and harvest, coming up!

Back in about April or May, while it was still cold and frosty, I planted 48 seeds in a little tray in my greenhouse. I would never have dreamed of the results of that simple and rather inexpensive little activity. As I watered them and kept the greenhouse warm with a little heater, I also watched as little tiny green sprouts appeared in each little container in the tray. As they grew and turned a rich deep green, I was not too surprised to find that they were what the seed packet said they would be: tomato plants. But I have been surprised — very pleasantly surprised — by the abundance and size of their fruit. And I only planted 36 plants in my garden. The rest I gave for others to grow.

I was almost overrun with tomatoes! There were certainly many more than we could use. Mary made 16 jars of tomato butter. She froze them by the bagful to use later in making fresh tomato sauce for our spaghetti meals in the middle of the winter. She also ate her share and gave at least five bushels of tomatoes to friends and staff at the Crossroads Centre. And all of this from just 36 tomato plants. As you can guess, I was totally happy with my tomato crop that year. The ancient Paul was right when he said in 2 Corinthians 9:6:

"...He who sows sparingly will also reap sparingly, and he who sows bountifully will also reap bountifully."

I have reaped bountifully. And others have benefited, too, by this rich harvest. One always has to plant seed to reap a harvest. There is a harvest, also bountiful, which is benefiting many people across Canada and around the world. It is a direct result of people, sometimes very sacrificially, planting seeds. It is a much more important harvest than tomatoes, or anything else in my gardens. Look at Psalm 126:6 with me:

"He who continually goes forth weeping, bearing seed for sowing, shall doubtless come again with rejoicing, bringing his sheaves with him."

Jesus told a parable about the sower and the seed, and He made a very clear statement about the seed. It's found in Luke 8:11:

"Now the parable is this: The seed is the Word of God."

The seed is the Word of God. The BIBLE is the Word of God. Jesus is the Living Word of God. The purpose of the Word being sown on the fields of the world is to bring an abundant harvest. And this harvest has two aspects: 1) that understanding and receptive hearts receive the Word of God and become children of God through the Living Word, Jesus Christ; and 2) that these same people have a growth and harvest of righteousness in their own lives, helping them become more like Jesus Christ. As a result, they will grow lush, full and bountiful. Look at Matthew 13:23:

"But he who received seed on the good ground is he who hears the Word and understands it, who indeed bears fruit and produces: some a hundredfold, some sixty, some thirty."

The bottom line in the Crossroads Ministry is not whether the bank balance is okay every month. The bottom line here is the harvest. Is it worth the time, effort and sacrifice of all those involved, including you? Is the harvest worthwhile?

The answer is a very simple, but emphatic YES! Look at 1 Peter 1:22-23:

"Since you have purified your souls in obeying the truth through the Spirit in sincere love of the brethren, love one another fervently with a pure heart, having been born again, not of corruptible seed but incorruptible, through the Word of God which lives and abides forever."

You see, this seed and its harvest, unlike my tomatoes, are forever!

DON'T WALK ON THE GRASS - YET

Spring is a good time of year to put up signs on your grass that say: "Don't walk on the grass"! A footprint on the soil, garden or grass will harden as it dries out and leave a permanent impression that could take a great deal of work to smooth out. There's a right and a wrong time to pull that heavy roller over your lawn. A certain amount of firmness needs to set in before you start working the *soil,* or even the *soul!*

In the spring, more snow is not anticipated, yet frost may come during the night. We can expect to see that beautiful, but not altogether welcome, haze of frost covering everything. It may even be that some flowers which have already grown up out of the ground will be frost-bitten and, as a result, plants will be ill-formed and damaged.

How we treat the lawn and gardens is important at this stage.

The frost leaves and the ground becomes very mushy. And it gets worse when it has been raining almost constantly. However, "April showers bring May flowers," along with grass, leaves on the trees, weeds and mud. That's natural!

The frost tends to heave and move a lot of things, including the level of the lawn. When little bumps form in the ground and strange hollows appear during the "frozen earth" period, it is good to put up a sign that says, "Stay Off The Grass." Otherwise, you'll have deep foot-prints in the grass that will harden into permanent depressions. As there is a right time to use a heavy roller to smooth out the lawn, there's also a wrong time. The wrong time is when the ground is too hard to push the bumps down or it's so mushy that it squishes ridges into the lawn.

Like the ground after a cold frost or heavy spring rain, new Christians need to be treated carefully too. Just after the frost of death has been eradicated by the warmth and presence of God's Son in their lives, they are very vulnerable. The joy of having lost their hardness of heart makes them very vulnerable to the footprints of all kinds of false doctrines and heresies that could jump in to try to form their think-ing.

I have a childhood friend who recently came to the Lord. He was carrying a book which he had read four times already. It was danger-ous, unbiblical material and I warned him not to swallow everything he reads and hears, unless it is fully supported by the Bible. At this stage he's vulnerable.

"Don't walk on the grass!" This is the time they need to be under the straight teaching of the Word of God, from a Bible-believing pul-pit, or a mature and Godly mentor.

Soon, that mushy impressionable period will pass, and they'll begin to firm up enough to take the big heavy roller as it passes over them. But for their own sakes, let them grow a bit of strength from the newly-indwelling Spirit of God and the power of the Word of God before you start shoving "your" particular convictions at them. "Keep off the grass" for a while. You could, even unintentionally, leave a deep footprint in their minds that may take years to level out. And they may never get over some of those wrong impressions!

"Stay off the grass"! The wisdom of your words cannot compare to God's Word and wisdom. Listen to Paul in 1 Corinthians 2:4-6a:

"And my speech and my preaching were not with persuasive words of human wisdom, but in demonstration of the Spirit and of power, that your faith should not be in the wisdom of men but in the power of God. However, we speak wisdom among those who are mature...."

Paul here is speaking to those who are mature. Now I'd like you to hear some advice given to those who are young in the faith; the impressional soil. Look at 1 Peter 2:1-2:

"Therefore, laying aside all malice, all guile, hypocrisy, envy, and all evil speaking, as newborn babes, desire the pure milk of the Word, that you may grow thereby."

Spend time in God's Word. That's where your convictions will harden and set, and you'll grow strong. But let me also warn you: There are people who would love to captivate your minds to their own way of thinking. They are generally opinionated and demanding. Beware of them. Listen to 2 Peter 3:17:

"You therefore, beloved, since you know these things beforehand, beware lest you also fall from your own steadfastness, being led away with the error of the wicked; but grow in the grace and knowledge of our Lord and Saviour Jesus Christ. To Him be the glory both now and forever. Amen."

You, who would be tempted to do it, "Don't Walk On The Grass." And you, who are new Christians, don't let anyone but God and His Word work on you!

YOU NEED PROTECTION

Everyone will recognize an egg, right? Wrong. Not everyone will recognize what is considered an egg, but only has a soft pliable membrane around it, rather than a shell. These soft roly-poly things, in fact, start out like eggs. But they have a slight problem: no armour or shell — just porous, delicate skin, barely holding them together. No protection! How's your protection?

Some of the strangest things can happen in a henhouse. One rooster, for instance, can handle 25 hens. He rules them, protects them, and is the master of the roost. When he finds a delicacy, such as a bug or a worm, he gives a certain sound (I call it a "chicken chuckle") and the hens come running to share in the bounty.

When a flock is out in the yard, the rooster is the one who keeps his eyes peeled for any danger, real or imagined. He takes no chances. If a human comes walking around a corner of the barn, he immediately gives a sharp warning, and every hen jerks her head up and gives full attention. When a hawk flies over, he does the same thing and they run for cover. If a dog wanders too close, there is another warning. Just like any other society, chickens need protection. And when chicks are hatched, the hen protects them initially, but the whole flock "keeps an eye" on them, just to be safe.

A while ago, I became the grandfather of a beautiful newborn: Victoria Alexandra Bombay. Everyone in the family circle keeps an eye on her so that no danger comes near, especially her mother Karen. Any slight threat, and a quick word or motion protects Victoria.

But a strange thing sometimes occurs in a henhouse. Now, as everyone knows, eggs are laid in a chicken coop — usually in a nest prepared for just such an occurrence. And, as everyone knows, eggs all have shells, to both protect and preserve them, right? Well, not always. Sometimes an egg is laid with something less than a normal calcium shell: just a membrane.

That is what I call a soft-shelled egg. It's not much more than a slightly rough, tissue-like skin. It can be pressed for the skin is very pliable and vulnerable. A little bit too much pressure, and the egg is all over the place. There's not much you can do for it, except use it right away. An egg that is just a week or so old, laid with a soft, skinlike shell begins to shrink. We tried to preserve it, but the skin was so soft and porous that the egg within became dehydrated and shrivelled to a strange multi-cornered chunk. Every egg needs a proper hard shell. An egg with a proper shell will last for months and still be good if properly refrigerated.

Brand new Christians need protection too. They need a shell around them to keep them from the dangers of drying up, being broken, and cast aside. And a protection has been provided. But, unlike an egg, the Christian must take some initiative in putting on this protection. We are told exactly what protection we can have in Ephesians 6:13-17:

"Therefore take up the whole armour of God, that you may be able to withstand in the evil day, and having done all, to stand. Stand therefore, having girded your waist with truth, having put on the breastplate of righteousness, and having shod your feet with the preparation of the Gospel of peace; above all, taking the shield of faith with which you will be able to quench all the fiery darts of the wicked one. And take the helmet of salvation, and the sword of the Spirit, which is the Word of God."

God has provided a shell of protection for your safety and preservation. But it is up to you to believe God enough to use it. First, look at Psalms 121:7:

"The Lord shall preserve you from all evil; He shall preserve your soul."

The exercise of faith and obedience to the Word of God will bring the protection of God. Look at 2 Timothy 4:18:

"And the Lord will deliver me from every evil work and preserve me for His heavenly kingdom. To Him be glory forever and ever. Amen!"

Believe it! Obey it! As a child of God, you can put on the armour of God and can claim His protection and help when needed. You don't have to remain as helpless and hopeless as an egg without a proper shell: shrivelled and eventually useless.

THE GREAT DETECTOR

Walking out to the barn on a very dark night can be a challenge at times. You can't see the path. You can't see an outline of the barn against the sky. A slight bit of light behind you from the house is not quite enough. After all, there are deep shadows among the pines where even a skunk may be waiting with his tail raised. That's why my daughter bought a special Christmas gift for herself and gave it to me for Christmas. Let me shed some light on this.

On a dark night, it can sometimes be a tricky business walking out to the barn. If it's one of those extremely dark nights, you might find yourself tripping over a snow shovel, or even walking into a tree. Or the worst case scenario: a skunk! The walk to the barn at night may seem like a simple procedure, but it can be a bit treacherous without light.

My daughter Elaine, who is responsible for her goats, finds it a bit unsettling to have to walk to the barn when there's no light. So, she bought me just exactly what she wanted for Christmas. It's a motion detector which switches on two 150-watt floodlights. It detects the slightest movement and suddenly you're in the light.

Several times at night, our dogs have wandered into the range of its sensitivity causing the lights to come on. The sudden glare rivets them for a while, until they realize it's just light. Then they carry on sniffing whatever little trail they were following.

Our motion detector detects the slightest movement. It's a great device and, since I have it turned up to its most super-sensitive setting, it provides ample light to get to the barn. I couldn't help but think of a blinding parallel.

There are times in our lives as Christians when we are at a loss as to what to do. We're in the dark. Have you ever been there? Not knowing just what the Lord wanted you to do? Well, God's sensitive searchlight is turned on at the slightest motion from us. Look at Romans 8:27:

"Now He who searches the hearts knows what the mind of the Spirit is, because He makes intercession for the saints according to the will of God."

Not only does God search our hearts with his penetrating light, but He also reveals the deep things of God to us. We read in 1 Corinthians 2:10:

"...God has revealed them to us through His Spirit. For the Spirit searches all things, yes, the deep things of God."

God has graciously revealed to us His will and His ways through His Word, the Bible. He has also granted us the presence of His Spirit as our guide and teacher. But we have to walk in God's ways. When we do step off the path, God graciously points it out to us by revealing our sin under the searchlight of His Spirit. Look at how it was described for the children of Israel, back in Numbers 32:23:

"But if you do not do so, then take note, you have sinned against the Lord; and be sure your sin will find you out."

How much more meaningful become the words of King David when he says in Psalms 119:105:

"Your Word is a lamp to my feet and a light to my path."

The promise of God is that by His Spirit He will be sensitive to your personal, as well as corporate, walk with God. Such a promise is found in Psalms 32:8:

"I will instruct you and teach you in the way you should go; I will guide you with My eye."

We don't have to walk in darkness. We have the provision and promise of God that He will shed light on our path; that He will guide our steps; and that His eyes will be protectively watching over us at all times. He has promised to detect and deter us when we make any motions which might lead us out of the way He has planned for us. We need only to learn to be sensitive. And we can, as we find in 1 John 1:7:

"But if we walk in the light as He is in the light, we have fellowship with one another, and the blood of Jesus Christ His Son cleanses us from all sin."

A beautiful song, a prayer really, comes to mind: "Search me, oh God, and know my thoughts I pray. Try me, oh Saviour, know my heart I pray. See if there be, some wicked way in me...." And He will! Just make a move in His direction, and the light will come on.

THERE'S ALWAYS A LITTLE MORE DIRT

There's nothing quite like a good rain after a dry spell. It's refreshing, cooling and causes growth. I've also noticed something else over the past few years. The evidence of what I have learned is at the bottom of my rain barrels at the barn. But I would never have really noticed if my rain barrels were not white. It's hard to believe what sometimes comes with the rain.

The barn is a fair distance from our house and we don't have water piped out there. Since 50 hens and two goats need a lot of water every day, it would mean a long and weary walk several times a day. Since I like labour-savings devices, I devised a great labour-saving device. I placed fifty-gallon plastic drums under the down spouts of the barn roof to collect rain water.

So every day, the walk is short — from the rain barrel to the chickens' water trays. Even in the winter, there is enough sun on the steel roof to melt snow and fill the barrels. I carry it inside the coop where it doesn't freeze, then dump what I can't store inside the coop. In this way, I've always got an empty barrel to catch the next melting snow.

However, I've noticed something that's very consistent, both in the summer and winter. The rain water is seldom clean. And melted snow water is also never clean, clear water.

These rain barrels are pure white. Even after heavy rains for several days, the rain barrels have collected dirt on the bottom. Clean it out after a heavy rain, and the next rain brings more dirt from the roof of the barn. It seems that there's always something dirty in the air which settles on the roof, and then settles in the bottom of the rain barrels. Fortunately, the dirt settles, and the chickens and goats get the good clear water from the top of the barrel.

The dirt always seems to be there. You can clean the barrels over and over again. The roof always seems to have some more dirt to be washed off by the rain water into the barrels. It seems like a never-ending cycle. Dirty, clean, dirty, clean!

This is something like life. There's always something that needs to be washed out of our lives. We are like barn roofs, exposed to an atmosphere that is something less than pure. The roof keeps most of it out of the barn, but it has to be washed off by continual rains. The longer it is between rains, the greater the amount of dirt which collects in the bottom of the barrel.

That's why it's so essential as Christians to have a good bit of rain from heaven wash us clean every day. And what is that rain from heaven? It's mentioned by Paul in Ephesians 5:25-26:

"...Christ also loved the Church and gave Himself for it, that He might sanctify and cleanse it with the washing of water by the Word."

The Word of God is what makes us clean. Jesus explained this very clearly to His disciples in John 15:3:

"You are already clean because of the Word which I have spoken to you."

A daily rain of God's Word will wash us clean, and since we live in a very perverse and polluted atmosphere, we can collect a lot of dirt in our lives if we don't have a daily cleansing. Too long between a cleanup, and the cleanup becomes more difficult. Without the cleansing of God's Word in our lives, we become less and less productive, and His purposes in our lives are frustrated. But when His Word constantly cleanses us, it prospers the purposes of God in our lives. Look at Isaiah 55:10-11:

"For as the rain comes down, and the snow from heaven, and do not return there, but water the earth, and make it bring forth and bud, that it may give seed to the sower and bread to the eater, so shall My Word be that goes forth from My mouth; it shall not return to Me void, but it shall accomplish what I please, and it shall prosper in the thing for which I sent it."

I haven't had to carry water from the house to the barn for several years. There's always enough rain, both to wash the barn roof and to slake the thirst of my livestock.

And there's always enough in God's Word to both clean and satisfy you as well. But you've got to expose yourself to it before it can do you any good.

Chapter 3

We're All In The Same Barn, I Hope!

ROOTS

You can support them with both stakes and tomato frames, but if they don't have roots, they'll eventually fall over, either from a contrary wind or from the weight of their own fruit-growing prowess. It seems to me that those who developed some of the hybrid tomato plants or flowers forgot a major ingredient. Roots! But what's the good of a great harvest which falls into the mud because its roots are inadequate. It's the same with people!

When I saw the roots, I began to understand. I had planted my sunflowers in my greenhouse early in the spring. When the fear of frost was past, I put them in one of my gardens. They grew quickly and they grew tall. In fact, they are several feet above my head and now have these great and massive sunflowers, just loaded with a fresh growth of sunflower seeds. These sunflowers have been bred to really produce results. They have great heads on them.

Then I looked at my tomatoes. Great big beefsteak tomatoes. They, too, have been specially developed to produce like crazy, and with almost perfect growing weather. I have had tomatoes I only heard about in the past. Big, luscious and meaty tomatoes with fantastic flavour and a low acid content. Wow, who could ask for anything more?

I could! I could ask for a plant that has better roots. With both my sunflowers and my tomatoes, they yielded to the first wind. Without enough roots, they could not stand. They fell over, pulling much of their roots right out of the soil. Their roots didn't go deep enough, and all their breeding went to their heads.

Sounds a bit like a generation here in Canada that is just coming into its own. We have bred them, concentrating on results and appearances, and insisting on great heads. At the same time, we have neglected their character and didn't develop roots for them. And now, when a bit of a contrary wind blows across their path, they have no foundation and they fall flat tearing out what roots they do have. A rootless generation is a danger to the future of this nation. We have developed great heads, but have neglected the Source of life and the heart, something like my sunflowers and tomatoes. In both cases, it was the weight of their own success which caused their downfall.

My prayer for Canada is that this present upcoming generation will not get quite so highly developed in the head, without looking after the basics of life: the Roots — the very Source of strength. And the only resource I know that actually works for both the head and the heart is God Himself. My prayer is found in Ephesians 3:16-19:

"...that He [God] would grant you, according to the riches of His glory, to be strengthened with might through His Spirit in the inner man, that Christ may dwell in your hearts through faith; that you, being rooted and grounded in love, may be able to comprehend with all the saints what is the width and length and depth and height — to know the love of Christ which passes knowledge; that you may be filled with all the fullness of God."

That is strength! That will give you the power to stand no matter what wind blows against you, and no matter the weight of your own success. God knows the balance necessary between the head and heart. It is only through making Him a very clear part of your life that you'll be strong enough to handle both rough weather and exceptional success. In Colossians 2:6-7, we read a bit more that tells the same story:

"As you therefore have received Christ Jesus the Lord, so walk in Him, rooted and built up in Him and established in the faith, as you have been taught, abounding in it with thanksgiving."

Get your life rooted and grounded in Jesus Christ. You'll stand when others fall around you. When your roots are down deep in God, it won't matter too much whether the soil is baked by the sun, or turned to mush by the rain. Either way you'll stand.

Roots make all the difference.

FREE TO A GOOD HOME

Did you ever see the ads in the newspaper, "Free Kittens To Good Homes"? How do they know whether your home or mine is good? If God restricted the giving of children to good homes only, we wouldn't have as many children in society as we do. As a matter of fact, what does make a good home? What is the best environment for children growing up? Are kids and kittens similar?

We have had two litters of kittens born on our little acreage in the past. One was a litter of four kittens and the next one, five kittens. We have never had problems finding homes for kittens before. But for some reason, the tomcats have been especially busy this year, and there are literally scores of fine feline family friends available this year. The Society For The Prevention of Cruelty To Animals (SPCA) has pens full of them, and the newspapers have dozens of "Free Kittens To Good Homes" advertisements. We still have a surfeit of kittens at our house and as beautiful and well-trained as they now are, no "good homes" have turned up for them.

But I got thinking about this "free to good home" thing. I'm certain that no one will do a "home inspection" before they release a kitten to a new owner. But, on the other hand, they probably won't turn them over to someone they think might be a cat kicker. So what constitutes a "good home"? For a cat, it could be a barn with plenty of mice. Or, it could be a house with a couple of children who love little things and would look after them well.

There seems to be a desire on the part of those who brought these kittens safely through birth and the initial weeks of life, to insure that they continue to get some loving care. After all, they are "my" kittens, and I'd like to know they are well cared for. Little kittens are delicate little things.

And so are children! But the problem is they are free to any home. The economic or intellectual capacity of a couple is not the criteria for children being born. And whether or not they will abuse, beat and demean children does not stop them from being born into such a home. Alcoholic parents can have children as well as those from good homes. Unlike kittens which are free to good homes, children are free to any kind of home. There would be many less children born if God restricted their availability only to what He considered "good" homes.

So what is a good home for children? Well, since it is God who gives children freely, perhaps the best description of a good home should be what God's Word says about it. And the Bible does say a few things about families and relationships. Look at Titus 2:2-5:

"...the older men be sober, reverent, temperate, sound in faith, in love, in patience; the older women likewise, that they be reverent in behaviour, not slanderers, not given to much wine, teachers of good

things — that they admonish the young women to love their hus-
bands, to love their children, to be discreet, chaste, homemakers,
good, obedient to their own husbands, that the Word of God may not
be blasphemed."

Now this is all said within the context of the Church. And the
Church of all places on this earth should be a safe haven for children.
As we all know, it has not always been so.

But there is a verse that has, in my case, deeply affected my life and
my attitude to children. It is found in Mark 9:42:

"And whoever causes one of these little ones who believe in Me to
stumble, it would be better for him if a millstone were hung around
his neck, and he were thrown into the sea."

That's strong language! So even if you don't have a kitten, you probably do have children. And I suppose only you really know whether or
not your home is a "good" home. But the great joy of this situation is
that, even if you think it's NOT a good home, it doesn't have to stay
that way. Just like the Joshua of Biblical fame said, *"As for me, and my*
house, we will serve the Lord!" (Joshua 24:15).

And you can do that best by leaving your kittens at home, and
being in church as a family every Sunday. Your church home will
make your house home a good home.

CHICKS

I'd like to report that my 50 newly-hatched chicks are doing fine.
But I want you to know that I'm not standing over them supervising
them every minute. They're allowed to develop at their own rate,
with limited freedom at first, and lots of warmth and food. Slowly they
get a bigger and bigger area where they can be free. Certain limits are
imposed, but every provision is given, especially warmth. I think I
treat my chicks better than some people treat their teenagers.

There are 50 new inhabitants in the Bombay barn: newborns, or
should I say, "newly-hatched" baby chicks. They are just two weeks
old. There are 25 from one line (White Meat Rocks) and 25 from
another (Shaver Cross).

The white ones are for us to eat. Oh, stop it! Everyone eats chick-
en! The other 25 I'm going to feed. I'm going to feed them with the

idea that eventually they will feed me with eggs. And as long as they do, I'll keep feeding them. When they stop laying eggs... well... we can discuss that another time.

I always go out to the barn as soon as I can after getting home from the office. I have to check on the chickens, the goats, and the greenhouse (as it can get either too hot or too cold). When I got out to the barn last Thursday, I opened the little room where I have my chicks. To my surprise, several were already out of the box and running around the whole room. As soon as I came, they jumped and fluttered back into the heated box where I started them out: "home," if you like. They saw danger and they headed home. That's where the food, water and warmth is: home!

When they get out, they are much more free, have more space and can explore a little. But they can't get out of the room. If they did, they'd be dead meat in a hurry. We have hawks, foxes and cats in our neck of the woods. I have to protect them from these predators.

At the first sign of danger, they head back into the lighted box where they are always welcomed by the rest of the brood.

This is something like teenagers. Parents are often taken by surprise when their young teens jump out of the box and start exploring a little more widely in life. But they tend to keep home in mind and run there when in danger. That's where the food, water and warmth is. Or should I say, that's where it *should be.*

Now, I'm the guy who provides all the food, water and warmth for my chicks. As long as I do, they'll keep coming back. At the same time, I'll give them more and more freedom — even into the big wide yard when they're ready. And I think I'll know when they're ready more accurately than they will.

Again, like teenagers, parents have to give increasing amounts of freedom to their teens, but at a rate that is controlled, not careless! And all the while, continuing to provide food, water and warmth — particularly warmth. Without love to come home to, a false love will be found outside the nest. There are all kinds of predators out there who will make offers. That's why it's absolutely essential to give freedom to children in progressive increments, rather than in one great swoop.

Wisdom doesn't grow quite as fast as the body does. This is the reason why parents should provide food — both spiritual and intellectual — as well as just hot dogs. Here's a sample of food which any teen should hear. It's in Proverbs 4:26-5:1:

"Ponder the path of your feet, and let all your ways be established. Do not turn to the right or the left; remove your foot from evil. My son, pay attention to my wisdom; lend your ear to my understanding...."

When you feed the souls and minds of your children, and provide the warmth of both your love and God's love, no matter how far they wander away, they'll come home when tough times come. They will realize the errors of their ways and be humbled, just like the prodigal son. Look at Luke 15:18-19:

"I will arise and go to my father, and will say to him, 'Father, I have sinned against heaven and before you, and I am no longer worthy to be called your son. Make me like one of your hired servants.'"

Look after them right when they're young, and they will keep coming home!

I'M A PRODUCT OF MY PAST

I found a brief letter, written in 1908, which might explain why I'm into chickens, eggs and chicken food. It was a great surprise to find this note written to my grandfather, which I will let you read. The note was from a chicken farmer near St. Catharines, Ontario. I knew malaria could get into your blood, but... chickens!!? Give me a break! My destiny was set about 90 years ago!

One evening, I was looking through some old papers and records from past generations of the Bombay family. I found a little Bible that gave the birth date of my great-grandfather, as well as his sister, Jane. We've never been able to get a trace on the family line through this great-grandaunt, who lived as a child on Scugog Island. And since the present spelling of the name Bombay was originally either Bumby, Bumbey or something similar, we can't find a trace.

As you are all aware, most of us are a product of our past, not just genetically but physically, spiritually, and even characteristically. One of our verbal traditions says that our great, great-grandfather on my dad's side was a temperance preacher, and some think he was also a bishop in the Church of England. He sent his son to Canada in disgrace because he came home hopelessly intoxicated one night. His son then settled on Scugog Island near Port Perry and had two children, John and Jane. Well, I never met my grandfather John since he died even before my parents were married. But I found an interesting piece of paper. Here it is. It's dated, February 29, 1908. It reads:

Mr. John Bombay,
Dear Sir, having used your "Pride of Canada Poultry Food," I find it fills the bill as my hens were all dying one after another till I used your food. They are all well and started laying. I would recommend it to anyone who has hens.
I remain yours, J. B. Bradley

On the back of the note, in my father's handwriting it says, "Father developed an egg-laying meal that was very effective."

I had a great, great-grandfather who was a bishop in England and a grandfather who was into chickens! My father also had chickens and was a minister of the Gospel as well. I guess this is why both the ministry and the raising of hens comes quite naturally to me. Some might think that there's something in my genes that says, "Preach, Boy! Preach! And while you're at it, raise chickens...."

I think neither preaching the Gospel, nor raising hens comes through the genes. What I know to be a fact is that we are a product of the influences, teaching and circumstances of our past, both good and bad. We learn from our forefathers. It's just the natural and, perhaps, even supernatural progression of life. I find my evidence in Exodus 34:6-7:

"And the Lord passed before him and proclaimed, 'The Lord, the Lord God, merciful and gracious, longsuffering, and abounding in goodness and truth, keeping mercy for thousands, forgiving iniquity and transgression and sin, by no means clearing the guilty, visiting the iniquity of the fathers upon the children and the children's children to the third and the fourth generation.'"

The Apostle Paul noticed this trait of tradition and teaching at a spiritual level in his son of the faith, Timothy. We read in 2 Timothy 1:5 where Paul writes:

"...I call to remembrance the genuine faith that is in you, which dwelt first in your grandmother Lois and your mother Eunice, and I am persuaded is in you also."

But something has happened in the last several generations of our civilization, at least in North America. Perhaps it's best described in Proverbs 30:11:

"There is a generation that curses its father, and does not bless its mother."

We are probably that generation. Look around you. I think it's time that parents and grandparents began to stick their noses into the lives of their offspring, and to regain some lost ground. We are urged by God in Deuteronomy 4:9 through Moses:

"...take heed to yourself, and diligently keep yourself, lest you forget the things your eyes have seen, and lest they depart from your heart all the days of your life. And teach them to your children and your grandchildren."

Raising chickens is neither here nor there when it comes to eternal matters, but providing a tradition of godliness and faith is an absolute essential. Morality and faith can't be legislated, but it can be taught by example and word.

GOD HAS ARRANGED IT SO

Don't you just love maple syrup? My neighbours have tapped a few trees in their back yard. They boil it down into syrup. Every spring someone sends us a litre or so of fresh maple syrup. What a taste on hot toast! But when I think of the tree that gave pails of sap to make syrup and yet still remains healthy, I marvel. Then there are the kind folk who share some of their syrup with us and still have plenty for themselves. God has arranged it so! Then I think of some folk who won't share anything with anyone. No wonder they shrivel! Perhaps God has arranged that too!

One day I was praying for the financial needs of the Crossroads Ministry. I looked across the woods to where my neighbour had tapped several sugar maples and saw the white pails hanging on the sides of the trees. It had been a cold night, and the sap had retreated into the roots. But during the day with the sun shining on the trunk and branches, the sap began to flow up again from the roots to give nourishment and new life to the buds forming on the extremities of all the branches. The buds were expanding slowly that spring because the cold lasted so long.

Every time the sun shines warmly, the sap begins to flow. I am amazed at the amount of sap that can be collected from a single sugar maple tree. Literally pails of it can be harvested, boiled down and used as maple syrup or maple sugar. But what amazes me even more is that no matter how much sap is drained off from the tree for people, there is always more than enough left for the tree to burst forth in beautiful new green leaves. God has arranged it so. Unless a tree is very badly abused and the bark is stripped off completely, there is always abundant life from the roots available to the branches and leaves. God has arranged it so!

Spring is a time of new life, refreshing warm breezes, and the retreating of cold air and cold temperature of the earth itself. Roots that have lain dormant all winter, wait for the sun, the warmth and the rains.

New life is so beautiful. Even new life in people is beautiful. When a person receives Jesus Christ as their Lord and Life, new energy begins to flow from that new life now rooted in God. As it says in Psalm 104:16a:

"The trees of the Lord are full of sap...."

And this new life is more than enough for the tree itself. God always supplies in abundance, but sometimes that abundance is wasted, unless it is shared. Look at how Daniel describes the trees in Daniel 4:12:

"Its leaves were lovely, its fruit abundant, and in it was food for all. The beasts of the field found shade under it, the birds of the heavens dwelt in its branches, and all flesh was fed from it."

"It was food for all...." If God supplies more than enough sap for a maple tree, is there some reason to doubt that he would supply less than enough for a Christian who has been planted in God?

Look at 1 Peter 1:3:

"Blessed be the God and Father of our Lord Jesus Christ, who according to His abundant mercy has begotten us again to a living hope through the resurrection of Jesus Christ from the dead."

This living hope needs to be shared. During Holy Week, when we celebrate the most amazing and proof-providing fact of history about the divinity of Jesus Christ — the resurrection — let's not be reticent about sharing the life that flows through us. We can do this both by telling and by supporting the "telling" of the truth of the Gospel. We have a commandment: *"Go into all the world, and preach the Gospel to every creature..."* (Mark 16:15). God's people need to share their abundant supply from God. Not just for the good of those who will receive new life, but for their own good. God blesses those who share their abundance. Look first at 2 Chronicles 31:5 where God's people received a command:

"As soon as the commandment was circulated, the children of Israel brought in abundance the firstfruits of grain and wine, oil and honey, and of all the produce of the field; and they brought in abundantly the tithe of everything."

And when God's people do share the heavenly flow of spiritual and material blessing that God gives them, there are genuine returns on such an investment. We go back to the analogy of the tree. Look at Psalms 1:3:

"He shall be like a tree planted by the rivers of water, that brings forth its fruit in its season, whose leaf also shall not wither; and whatever he does shall prosper."

Sounds good to me! God has arranged it so!

I NEED A TELEPHONE IN MY BARN

We've been having telephone problems at our house recently. It actually started on my birthday. One phone would begin chirping like a bird. Another time, all the phones went dead. Once, a friend on the other end of the line heard part of someone else's conversation, as well as our own. It can be disconcerting when you're cut off or only have occasional connections. Obviously, something had to be fixed. And I had to take the initiative!

I was thinking how convenient it would be to have a telephone in the loft. Several times, while recording commentaries up there, we have run into technical glitches and have had to telephone a studio engineer at Crossroads to get some help. My portable phone just doesn't reach as far as the barn. I also feel rather silly asking the production crew (still in the loft) questions from the middle of my back yard, then having to yell instructions back up to them.

You'd think with all the "state-of-the-art" communications we have at the Crossroads Centre, we'd be able to communicate better. After all, we are in the communications business. There's just one problem. We have another agency between my loft and the studios. It's called the telephone company.

Recently, we've had some real problems communicating even from the house. One night, one of our telephones chirped like a bird most of the night. At other times, we'd get strange rings and would answer the phone, only to hear static. Sometimes it would work again for a while. Then it would rain, which seemed to have a detrimental effect on our lines. Other times, I would have a dead phone in my hand only to hear heavy breathing in my ear. Just when I thought, Oh, it's one of those calls... I suddenly realized it's my own breathing sounds feeding back into the earpiece. So I ended up talking to myself, to make sure it was my own breathing, of course.

Well, I called the telephone company. They asked all the usual questions. Then they decided, among other things, that it was my portable phone. "Please leave it unplugged for 24 hours," they advised. We did. Sure enough, our little pink telephone chirped most of the night, and then the system went dead again. So, I called the telephone company a second time. They insisted it was the portable phone, even though it was not even connected. Finally, they agreed to send someone out to "check the lines." Strange, as that's what I was asking for from the beginning!

Somehow or other, something had come between our home and everyone we wanted to talk to. Modern technology is great, if it works!

Now, at Christmas time, we often have interruptions between ourselves and the One we want to communicate with. Oh, I'm not meaning our communication with friends and family. That usually increases. I'm talking about our communication with God. The Christmas frenzy seems to short out the time we would normally spend in prayer, talking to Him. The weather, activity, decorating, shopping, wrapping and a zillion other things rain down on us and seem to short out our line with God. And all of this happens at Christmas time, when the Lord should be the absolute centre of our attention and communication.

Can I make a suggestion? Take "time out" with God every day, every Christmas. You may just find that the frenzy subsides and the activity much less hectic. In Peter's sermon on the day of Pentecost, he said in Acts 2:28:

"You have made known to me the ways of life; you will make me full of joy in Your presence."

But that's only when the lines of communication are open. And Peter didn't mean just when you get on your knees or pick up the telephone, so to speak. It means a continually open line, when your mind is ALWAYS open to God. Listen to what is said in Isaiah 26:3:

"You will keep him in perfect peace, whose mind is stayed on You, because he trusts in You."

So, every Christmas, don't let the lines go dead between yourself and the Jesus of Christmas. In fact, get together with a few hundred other fellow Christians and worship and praise together. David says in Psalms 52:9:

"I will praise You forever, because You have done it; and in the presence of Your saints I will wait on Your name, for it is good."

On the other hand, that's about the only time of the year some people open up the lines between themselves and God. What a pity.

By the way, thanks to our telephone technician, Lyle. The phones are working now!

THERE'S NOTHING MORE SATISFYING

Christmas is a time for friends and family. I have quite a few friends and actually I count you among them, even though I may not have met you personally yet. (I hope we'll meet some day — in heaven, for sure!) Anyway, some of my best friends are at home: Mary, my family, and well, yes, I'll say it... my chickens! You can't imagine how relaxing it is when you're with a bunch of friendly clucks like I have at home!

One of my special joys is to collect the eggs when I get home in the evening. I usually put on the same red plaid barn jacket. The chickens have become used to it. When I wear something else, they act wary and very skittish. When they see that big human figure coming in slowly and easily, wearing that red jacket, they have no fear.

They've come to trust me. When I come in, they know that I'm not a danger — I'm not going to bite their heads off. They gather around my feet clucking away contentedly. Sometimes they are so close and friendly, I have to wade through them slowly, almost like wading through water. Otherwise, I'd probably step on them.

There's nothing more satisfying than hearing that contented clucking and chirruping as they wander around at my feet. I carefully reach in for the eggs. And even when a hen is on the nest, she lets me reach under her to gather those nice low-cholesterol products: firm, brown, medium-sized eggs. I'm speaking of the brown hens at the moment. The white hens, well, they are another story as they are always scattering, skittish and scared.

One of the brown hens follows me around so faithfully and doggedly that she actually gets in the way. I'm not too sure what's in that little pea-sized brain of hers, but she seems to feel it necessary to jump up to the nearest roost near the nests, and watch me collect every egg. She may even be counting them, I don't know. She does seem to be more intelligent than a chicken should be.

It's rather satisfying to have those few moments of clucking and crowded friendliness every evening. It's a happy, relaxing atmosphere. It's the kind of thing that every city dweller should experience from time to time. It's a reminder that life isn't just a mass of speed and sound; car and computers; work, sweat and grime. (Well, let's strike out that word "grime," since there is an essence of grime involved.) But if you can discount the smell (which I don't even notice anymore), a healthy and happy chicken coop isn't the worst place on earth. Being among friends, even if they are chickens, is a good thing.

I've heard it said, "The more people I meet, the more I like my dogs!" Obviously that person has met the wrong people. And from time to time, I must admit I'd prefer my chickens to some of the clucks I've met. But most people are nice, and especially so the more you get to really know them. What would life be like without friends? Job had friends who really wanted to help, but they really didn't stick with him too well; nor did his family. Listen to Job 19:14:

"My relatives have failed, and my close friends have forgotten me."

Job was a man with integrity, because he did not forsake the friends who had forsaken him. Listen to Job 42:10:

"And the Lord restored Job's losses when he prayed for his friends. Indeed the Lord gave Job twice as much as he had before."

However, you've got to be careful who you choose as friends. It says in Proverbs 12:26:

"The righteous should choose his friends carefully, for the way of the wicked leads them astray."

And again in Proverbs 18:24:

"A man who has friends must himself be friendly, but there is a friend who sticks closer than a brother."

It may be that over this past year, you have lost a good friend through something that came between your friendship. It doesn't matter whose fault it may have been. That's basically irrelevant. Perhaps at this time of year you should take an initiative and show yourself friendly. A friend regained is a friend who will remain.

Christmas is a time for friendships to be made, or remade. And there is a Friend who sticks closer than a brother. Have you met Him? Here's a hint: He came that first Christmas for you. Make friends with Him. He will never disappoint you!

How else can Christmas have any real meaning to you?

EGGS JUST DON'T HAPPEN, YOU KNOW!

Not everything that happened to me over the Christmas holidays was painful. Just my back. But some things have got to be done, whether I feel good or not. I have to feed and water my chickens and, of course, collect the eggs. I like taking up the collection. Was I surprised when I took up the collection on December 30th! What an offering — eggs, that is....

Eggs just don't happen you know! There's a great deal of work that goes into the making of an egg. The main burden lies on the shoulders of the hen. But there's more to it than just that. They must have a good solid diet with about 17 percent protein and any extra grubs, bugs, worms and flies that can be caught. Then they need to have enough calcium in their diet to be able to form a strong enough shell to hold it all together until it reaches its destiny.

Even though I fell down the stairs just before Christmas and hobbled around rather painfully, there are some responsibilities I simply wouldn't budge on; that is, caring for my chickens and, even more importantly, collecting the eggs. In fact, my hens have been a little behind schedule in their giving for the past few months.

On one occasion when I collected the eggs, I found a weird thing in the nest. Now you know the normal size of an egg. But this time? It's hard to believe a chicken made it. A hummingbird maybe!

This reminds me of when I was just a child in North Bay, Ontario, and my dad was pastoring a church. The offerings were about the same size. My dad kept records of all his financial affairs. One year, his average salary was $1.37 a week. Well, we survived, all four of us at that time; but just survived.

Then the next day I went out again to collect the eggs, gingerly making my way along the icy path to the barn. The opposite was true, I have never seen a larger chicken egg in my life.

In spite of my sore back, I almost ran back to the house to show Mary. I said, "It's almost as if one of those hens had a guilty conscience about her poor performance for the last few months." So, before the end of the year (while she could still get her tax credits for giving), she decided to go all out and produce an outstanding love offering. Now chickens don't get tax credits, of course; but, on the other hand, that's not why they give. They give eggs because it's their nature.

Why do you give? For tax credits? But giving isn't restricted to simply material things like eggs or money. Look at Romans 12:6-8:

"Having then gifts differing according to the grace that is given to us, let us use them: if prophecy, let us prophesy in proportion to our faith; or ministry, let us use it in our ministering; he who teaches, in

teaching; he who exhorts, in exhortation; he who gives, with liberality; he who leads, with diligence; he who shows mercy, with cheerfulness."

You should hear the cheering that takes place when a hen lays an egg. Every chicken in the coop joins in the rejoicing, no matter who lays the egg! But giving should not be unduly announced. Look at Matthew 6:1:

"Take heed that you do not do your charitable deeds before men, to be seen by them. Otherwise you have no reward from your Father in heaven."

So, when you send your gift in to *100 Huntley Street*, just quietly slip it into an envelope, seal it, and our close-mouthed mail readers will keep quiet about it.

As I thought of those two chickens, and the size of their "gifts," I had another thought: they gave what they had, big or small! Look at what Paul says in 2 Corinthians 8:12:

"For if there is first a willing mind, it is accepted according to what one has, and not according to what he does not have."

Well, when my chickens started producing more eggs for me, and most of them are big, I decided to do a bit better for them too. Because of their bounty, I decided to increase their bounty. I turned up the heater in the chicken coop to make them more comfortable. That's Biblical too. Look at 2 Corinthians 9:6:

"But this I say: He who sows sparingly will also reap sparingly, and he who sows bountifully will also reap bountifully."

And God does that for us too. When we give to Him, He turns up the comfort level in our lives. He blesses us. He provides for us, usually beyond our expectations!

Chapter 4

Welcome To The Barn

PESTS ASIDE

When my cherries were eaten by robins, I knew I had a problem. Then when I found out that the blue jays were eating holes into my apples as soon as some red began to appear, I knew I had even more problems. But the final straw was when the raccoons began decimating my corn. Whoever said farming was fun should take a look at my corn patch. But there is a way! There is a way to put the pests aside, and I'm not talking only about pesticide! Come, visit me in my garden!

No one can know the hours I have spent in the late evenings in my three vegetable gardens — tilling, planting, weeding, watering and waiting. I even sprayed a few things with pesticide so that we would not accidentally bite into more protein than we were counting on. I think cabbage has enough protein without the extra provided by those three-quarter inch long, green wiggly things. So, I put those pests aside, with a pesticide.

When the gardens are just coming into their own, there are lots of tomatoes, many over five inches across; okra, green and lovely; cucumbers, which Mary likes; Swiss chard; carrots; peas; squash; pumpkin; watermelon; cantaloupe; and raspberries. And the corn! Oh, the corn! I love corn on the cob.

But some of my neighbours thought I was growing the corn for them. Oh, I don't mean my human neighbours, but the ones who live in the bushes and trees down by the river. Raccoons and, of all things, opossum. And it's a strange thing about these animals; these pests. They like corn too. But they like it before it gets a bit too tender, about three or four days before it's really ready for human consumption. It reminded me of how foxes go for the tender grape vines, ruining the crop before it is anywhere near ready. Have you ever read about that? There's a reference in a 3,000-year-old song about it. It is in Song of Solomon 2:15:

"Catch us the foxes, the little foxes that spoil the vines, for our vines have tender grapes."

So, I decided to catch the raccoons that were spoiling my corn. I rented a live trap. Well, my first catch was a neighbour's cat. I let him go. Then it was our own cat. I let him go. Then it was our own dog.

Well, I let her go too, since she had to rush back to the house to feed her new pups. Well, my fortunes changed. I got two raccoons and two opossum. I caught the pests, and put these pests aside. And now my peaches-and-cream corn is being eaten by the "cob-load" — by us! It's sweet and snappily fresh. Where once there was ruin and waste, now there is life and health. It's typical of life, isn't it?

Even my apple trees are suffering from similar thieves. As soon as some red appears on the apples, the blue jays peck great holes in them, eating a bit and causing the rest to rot. They, too, seem to get to the apples just shortly before they are ready to harvest. Earlier, our cherry tree was under attack by robins. We threw a net over that tree and protected the harvest. There always seems to be something out there that will try to steal and ruin what should be wholesome and come to full fruit — yes, even in our own lives. Just like these devilish little thieves who try to cash in on my hard work in the garden, the real devil will try to suck the best out of your life and mine. Look at John 10:10:

"The thief does not come except to steal, and to kill, and to destroy. I have come that they may have life, and that they may have it more abundantly."

There is only one pesticide that defeats the devil. That is when you throw a protective net around your life by trusting in the power of the shed blood of Jesus Christ. Nothing else works. If you want the best out of life, and the abundance that God originally intended when He planted you in this life, you've got to be out of the thief's reach. And the only place possible is when, as it says in Colossians 3:3:

"...your life is hidden with Christ in God."

You can take care of that right now by calling on God through Jesus Christ and asking Him to forgive your sins, and come in to control and protect your life. I suggest you do this before your life is in complete ruins at the hands of the thief.

A TIME TO REAP

I can hardly wait to get my Rototiller into my gardens in the spring. The famous Onondaga clay is very sensitive to wet and dry. If the top is wet, you bog down; too dry and it's like trying to Rototill bricks.

There's a right time for planting and a right time for weeding; a right time for sun and rain; and, most importantly, a right time for harvest. If you miss the harvest, all the rest was wasted effort. The harvest *always* comes and, even if it is meagre, it can't be wasted.

Farmers are at high pitch on the land in the spring. The winter is spent repairing and making most of the machinery ready for the work in the fields. Hours are spent replacing worn parts, cleaning and making sure everything is in working order. And the fields are waiting and drying out just enough to work; but not so dry that the soil blows away in the wind or becomes too hard to work.

First comes ploughing (and harrowing when necessary), making sure the weeds are turned under deep enough to die and enrich the soil but not so shallow that they come up again as weeds. Then comes the planting. After this is the need to patiently wait for the right amount of rain and sun. Farming is a very demanding calling. And, at the end of the summer, harvest time! That's the big and final payoff: food for months to come, income for the needs of life and new parts for the machinery needed for next year's crop.

It's an awful thing to miss the harvest. All that work, patience, watering, waiting, weeding could be totally wasted if you miss the harvest. The harvest is what it is all about. Your timing has to be very precise. Every different crop has its own best time for harvest. For example, you have to make hay when the sun shines! And so it is with the great spiritual harvest. Every different person has a perfect time to be harvested into the kingdom of God.

Recently, I felt a nudge from the Spirit of God to talk to a young lady who had been assigned to work at *100 Huntley Street* in our TV production department for a month or so by her college. I asked her if she had ever accepted Jesus Christ into her life as Lord and Saviour. It appeared that she had not, and within a few minutes she had accepted Jesus Christ as her Lord and Saviour. I had no idea at the time that it was her last day to be with us at *100 Huntley Street*. God's timing is perfect. Likewise, there is a right time for the harvest.

Two days previously, a woman of 82 years came to me for prayer for a medical problem. I felt strongly to ask her if she had ever accepted Jesus as her own personal Lord and Saviour. She had not. She also prayed the sinner's prayer and accepted Jesus as her Saviour. Afterwards, I prayed for the healing of her sickness. First things first! Once again, God's time of harvest is perfect.

What if, in both of these cases, I had not listened to that still small voice within? What if I had missed the harvest of both of these lives? What if the harvest had passed, and they were not saved? All the preparation, praying, watering, weeding and readiness in their lives could have passed irrevocably?

The frustration of preparing and planting my gardens has often driven me almost to tears, but then there is the harvest. Look at Psalm 126:5:

"Those who sow in tears shall reap in joy."

Nothing can duplicate my joy when that young lady accepted Jesus into her heart. Nothing in all the world can duplicate my joy when that 82-year-old lady found that God could live inside her through Jesus Christ!

But you have to sow before you can reap. Listen to Hosea 10:12:

"Sow for yourselves righteousness; reap in mercy; break up your fallow ground, for it is time to seek the Lord, till He comes and rains righteousness on you."

In Ecclesiastes 3:2, we read that there is:

"A time to be born, and a time to die; a time to plant, and a time to pluck what is planted."

We are sowing continually through *100 Huntley Street*, and you've helped us. But God wants you to be involved in the reaping too. Have you ever asked anyone if they watch *100 Huntley Street*, and used that as an opportunity to invite them to receive Jesus as Lord and Saviour? This is of utmost importance, because there is a time to die.

Don't say, "Four months, then comes the harvest. Lift up your eyes... the harvest is right beside you!

IT CAN'T BE DONE ALONE

Planting potatoes is a back-breaking job. Soil has to be prepared and a hole dug, into which the potato will be gently placed. But if the potatoes (like the ones Mary discovered in our pantry) try to grow without soil (never finding a place to put their roots), they'll eventually consume themselves and then rot away. Have you recognized any-one recently, acting like a potato?

I was planting a few potatoes quite early the other morning, since I had to drive up near Ottawa that day for a men's retreat. These pota-toes had been sitting in the pantry for a few weeks. Even in the dark of the pantry they had somehow sensed it was spring, and that it was time to grow — time to come to life.

They had grown little sprouts about two or three inches long, and had begun to draw on their own inner resources to send out these lit-tle shoots. Normally, the shoots turn green and, as a result of the sun, pour down energy into the roots so they could bear fruit. There was only one problem though: they had no place to develop roots. If left alone, they would simply suck all the resources out of themselves, then wither, die, and go rotten.

So, I did them a favour and myself, too, I guess. I took them out to the one garden where I have soft enough soil to grow root vegetables and gently settled them into the ground, covering the shoots with moist earth. The day would be sunny. Growth would continue. They had some place now to put down their roots. Now they could fulfil that genetic inner urge to come to life and actually take root, grow and bear fruit.

I couldn't help but think of some people who try to be like Christians, without becoming Christians. Let me explain...

I have met people who have this strong inner urge to be useful; to make their lives worthwhile. They draw on all their inner resources and actually start showing some of the characteristics of Christians, such as kindness, honesty, integrity and neighbourly love. And, if they're really big potatoes, they can go on in this way for a long time. But eventually they become disillusioned and even bitter because they have nothing to replace all they have drawn out of their own resources. To be a Christian and to have the resources to maintain the strength and growth of good fruit, you need to be part of something bigger than yourself. Jesus said it this way in John 15:4:

"Abide in Me, and I in you. As the branch cannot bear fruit of itself, unless it abides in the vine, neither can you, unless you abide in Me."

Death, and finally rottenness, awaits a potato that never finds roots. So it is with the person who wants to be a Christian, but doesn't put down roots in Jesus Christ. The apostle speaks of these people in 1 Peter 1:23 as:

"...having been born again, not of corruptible seed but incorruptible, through the Word of God which lives and abides forever."

If that is where you are (trying to exhibit all the characteristics of a Christian without actually becoming a Christian), then my prayer for you is the same as the one Paul prayed for the Ephesians, in Ephesians 3:16-19:

"...that He would grant you, according to the riches of His glory, to be strengthened with might through His Spirit in the inner man, that Christ may dwell in your hearts through faith; that you, being rooted and grounded in love, may be able to comprehend with all the saints what is the width and length and depth and height — to know the love of Christ which passes knowledge; that you may be filled with all the fullness of God."

That way, there are no illusions. That way, there is real life, drawn from a resource other than yourself; a divine Source.

Living the Christian life without being rooted and grounded in His love is very difficult and, in the end, quite impossible. The potato will just become corrupt.

May I offer some advice? Don't abandon the good things you are trying to do. Something in your very nature is calling you to put out those little shoots of life and growth. But you better get what you need from Jesus. If you don't, you'll end up alone... corrupted... without eternal roots.

Why not ask God to help you get planted in Jesus Christ right now. You need those roots in fertile soil.

YOU JUST CAN'T TOP IT!

Have you ever been there, where you had planted a seed, such as a bean, and actually saw the soil move a little as the slight, but persistent, life of new growth pushes its way out of the ground? It can be an awesome experience. Have you planted any seeds this year? Have you ever experienced the thrill of seeing real, new, tender life start as a result of seeds you have sown? And I'm not just talking about a hill of beans!

We have gardens at our house. Mary and Elaine take the main bulk of the responsibility in the flower gardens, although once in a while I get involved in putting in the bulkier stuff. Mary has about a dozen different flower gardens scattered around our yard. Elaine also has an herb garden with all kinds of nice-smelling and savoury-tasting things.

Although a lot of our stuff was started in a little greenhouse I built, a lot of seed is sown directly into the gardens. As you probably know, the little seed packages tell you how long you will have to wait for germination. Corn, for example, takes seven to ten days; carrots, up to three weeks; and so on.

I have never been known for an overdose of patience. I go out the day after I plant seeds and look to see if anything is happening. Even though I know corn won't show before six or seven days at best, yet I somehow am disappointed when three days later, there's still nothing showing above ground. When you've invested seed into the ground, you want to know that it's going to be worth the investment of time, the price of the seed, and the careful preparation of the soil. So every day, as soon as I can get into my rough and, perhaps, tacky clothes (which I call my "grubbies"), I head for the garden to see what's happening.

What a thrill it is, when you see that first little green sprig of life easing out of the earth. When I saw my first bean plant just breaking the soil and unbending into growth above ground, I smiled with joy. After all, this was seed I had planted! This was seed I had a very personal interest in. This was a new little green life that I had a hand in.

Bean plants are so tender and vulnerable at the beginning. A cat stepping on them can snap them off, and it's all over. A rabbit can drop by for a snack, and that's that! And it's amazing how protective I get about those neat little rows of beans, beets and future salads I grow. I walk on the weeds with impunity because all they do is weaken and rob the soil which I want my plants to be nourished by.

Have you ever had the simple, yet profound, joy of watching something you planted come to life and start reaching for the sun? I have! And I love it! But even more thrilling is when I see a person (in whom

I have had a hand in planting the seed of the Word of God) suddenly break the surface of this earth's dirt. What a thrill to watch as they grow and mature in the things of God! What a delight! Look again at Psalm 126:6:

"He who continually goes forth weeping, bearing seed for sowing, shall doubtless come again with rejoicing, bringing his sheaves with him."

I know that sense of rejoicing when it comes to growing things in my garden. But there is a greater thrill in my life when I have helped bring life to a newborn babe in Christ. Although I have no way of knowing the labour pains of a mother on the verge of giving birth to a child, I certainly know the effort and labour (and the patient waiting) as the Word of God takes root in an eternal soul. The apostle compares it to just such an event in John 16:21:

"A woman, when she is in labour, has sorrow because her hour has come; but as soon as she has given birth to the child, she no longer remembers the anguish, for joy that a human being has been born into the world."

When you are sowing the seed and praying for the results, it can include anguish. But, oh the joy when a person breaks out of the darkness into the light. Have you ever had that experience? Have you ever led a person into life in Jesus Christ? Have you ever seen new life come into being right before your eyes?

It's fabulous! You just can't top it!

THERE'S CLEAN SOIL AND DIRTY SOIL!

I've had three loads of topsoil delivered to my house over the past few years. The first load, well, I was taken for a ride. It was just junky, rocky, lumpy waste. It wasn't at all what I really wanted. But the second load was perfect, clean, workable, and exactly what I needed. Recently, I had another load delivered. Naturally, I went to the source of the good stuff. Once you've had the good stuff, you'll never ever want the junk again.

There's nothing quite like the feel of good soil sifting through your fingers. Where I live, we don't really have the best soil in the world. Although it's very fertile, it's clay soil. When it dries, it's a bit like trying to sift bricks through your fingers. It's rough, hard, difficult to work, and almost impossible for root vegetables. It has to be worked and broken up just at the right time. Too soon, and the Rototiller just bogs down, sinking lower and lower into thick mud. Too late, and the Rototiller leaps all over the place trying to break its way through the hardened clay soil.

So, for my gardens, I decided to buy a load of loamy soil to mix with the clay in order to soften and lighten it up a bit. I phoned a local trucker and had a truckload delivered. I had it dumped right in the middle of my big vegetable garden. Then I tried to spread it out and Rototill it into the clay soil. It was full of tree roots, hard clay lumps and stones — so many stones.... It was difficult to work, but I finally got it spread out, mixed in, and planted.

A few weeks later, I had more weeds than I had before in my garden and they were a kind I had not seen on my property before. I had actually imported "dirty" dirt. It was full of weed seeds, stones and roots, and my garden soon became a greater challenge than ever before.

The next time I needed a load of soil, I was more careful. I asked around a bit. I phoned a few contractors and asked them some questions, such as, "Where is this soil coming from?" and "What was grown in it before?" You learn a few things the longer you live. Well, I finally settled on a supplier. That first load was beautiful, weed-free, and has improved every garden I've added it to. Later on, when I needed another load, you don't even have to guess where I phoned to get a delivery. Again, beautiful top soil; clean, without old roots and stones mixed in it. When you find a good source, you stick with it.

People have similar problems when they are looking for answers in life. They scan the yellow tabloids or their TV screens. When they come across something that sounds like what they need, they try it. Then they buy the whole load. Suddenly life becomes an even greater challenge and disappointment than before. Perhaps it was alcohol, or drugs, or those personal ads in the newspaper. Perhaps it was the trip of a lifetime, or a guru, or hypnotist that claimed to be able to get right to the core of your life's problem. And the source turns out to be all wrong. Life becomes even more complicated with more questions than answers.

I'd like to offer a suggestion. Ask around a bit more. Find out where there is a good source; where you can count on a good, clean, helpful and full load of answers. In fact, I'd suggest you go to the Source: God Himself. Jesus told people who are looking for something good, clean, and satisfying in life to:

"Come to Me, all you who labour and are heavy laden, and I will give you rest. Take My yoke upon you and learn from Me, for I am gentle and lowly in heart, and you will find rest for your souls" (Matthew 11:28-29).

God, your Creator is the Source of all good things. When He supplies what you need (and He is able to supply *all* your need), it will not be loaded with roots, rocks and weeds. It will be a clean load. Listen to Philippians 4:19:

"And my God shall supply all your need according to His riches in glory by Christ Jesus."

There's clean stuff and dangerous dirty stuff available out there. You have to make the choice. Just be careful what you try.

THE SPIDER

Have you ever really noticed spiders? I'm told our spiders here in Canada are not too dangerous and that very few of them are really poisonous. Try telling that to a fly or a small moth! Common, simple, nicely-coloured garden spiders are lethal to their victims. They don't build their webs to catch human beings. But there is someone who has all the bad characteristics of the spider, plus a few more, who would love to trap you in his web.

One summer day as I was writing some of my commentaries, I noticed a very large spider just outside the window. He was working energetically back and forth, using one of the frames of the window as an anchor for attaching his web. Back and forth he went, up and down and then in circles, connecting and strengthening the web. It was fascinating to watch.

The glass was clean and, to the casual eye, you wouldn't even notice the rather intricate web he had put in place. When he was finished building his web, he retreated up under the dark side of the upper window frame. Now even he was invisible to the casual glance. He waited. He was waiting for something to devour. A fly perhaps, or maybe a small moth. He waited. So did I, for a while. Then I went back to the job at hand: writing a commentary. But, every once in a while, I would glance up and peek under the window frame to see if that fat spider was still there. He was. Patient and deadly.

Finally, just as I glanced out the window, a fly flew right into the web and in a flash the spider was on him, gave him a lethal injection, then started wrapping the fly in grave clothes: a tightly wound web. One more victim of a lethal enemy who would eagerly devour his prey.

How like the one we know as Satan. Peter makes an even more ferocious comparison. Listen to what he says in 1 Peter 5:8:

"Be sober, be vigilant; because your adversary the devil walks about like a roaring lion, seeking whom he may devour."

Unlike the spider, Satan is out on the prowl; but like the spider, he will victimize anyone who gets into his web. And the unsuspecting often bring it on themselves, by the way they live and, sometimes, even by their treatment of other people. Look at 2 Peter 2:12-14 with me:

"But these, like natural brute beasts made to be caught and destroyed, speak evil of the things they do not understand, and will utterly perish in their own corruption, and will receive the wages of unrighteousness, as those who count it pleasure to carouse in the daytime. They are spots and blemishes, carousing in their own deceptions while they feast with you, having eyes full of adultery and that cannot cease from sin, beguiling unstable souls. They have a heart trained in covetous practices, and are accursed children."

Just like an unwary fly can be caught in a spider's almost invisible web, so people can be caught in activities and habits which initially have no visible dangers. But the end is a lethal injection, and eternal grave clothes.

We are warned to stay away from these kinds of people because they, already totally immersed in a corrupt form of lifestyle, will try to rationalize and justify their own sins. They can be very convincing as they try not just to make themselves appear acceptable, but to entice others into the same depraved and godless lifestyle. This is one of the great dangers of accepting human philosophy as opposed to the truth of God as it is expressed through the life, teaching, death and resurrection of Jesus Christ. Listen to Paul's solemn warning in Colossians 2:8:

"Beware lest anyone cheat you through philosophy and empty deceit, according to the tradition of men, according to the basic principles of the world, and not according to Christ."

There is one and only one safe way to go through life. And that is brilliantly expressed in the Scriptural record of the life and teachings of Jesus Christ. Sin and righteousness are clearly demarcated. The difference between eternal life and eternal punishment is shown. And present righteousness as well as the way to eternal life are displayed so simply that even a child can escape the destroyer who, like the spider, wants only to kill and devour. And here is the way:

"...if you confess with your mouth the Lord Jesus and believe in your heart that God has raised Him from the dead, you will be saved" *(Romans 10:9).*

The only other choice is the spider — and his eternal, lethal injection!

INSIDE, LOOKING OUT

Freedom is a wonderful thing! I watched a robin — free as only a bird can be — finding and pecking worms out of the lawn. The robin was perfectly natural and free to be what it was created to be. Then I saw a hawk circling in the sky, free to plunge to earth for that mouse or snake, and simply be what it was meant to be. Afterwards, I saw some ladybugs trapped inside my loft window, without any hope of freedom, except one little crack in the wall.

Freedom is a wonderful thing!

As I sat writing this commentary, I was looking out the window in my loft and was amazed to see scores of ladybugs crawling around on the panes of glass. Some would even take flight for a little while. Somehow they seemed larger than life and looked as though they were free and enjoying themselves. But in every single case, they'd fly back toward the window, whack into it with what must have been some degree of discomfort and fall to the window ledge, just to start crawling again.

When they were flying, some got as high as the ceiling. Some flew in circles, away from the window. Unfortunately, they were attracted to a big 300-watt bulb and were burnt when they hit it. But when they hit the window, they crawled around in what seemed a desperate attempt at getting past the glass and out into the free air. They were trying to get out into their natural surroundings which was really supposed to be their normal habitat. Outside, there is everything they need to survive, including aphids and small mites which constitute their healthy diet. Inside is dust, a few dead flies, and very little else to feed on.

I felt sorry for them. They were not fulfilling the purpose for which God had created them. They were confined, trapped and restricted. Although they could see freedom, they didn't have access to it — at least, not until I got them to a crack in the window frame through which they could go. Some crawled through to freedom. But I had to show most of them the way. Some never made it, and their little orange corpses lay lifeless and still on the window ledge.

Freedom is a wonderful thing for people too!

And just like the beautiful little ladybugs, people flit around for a while looking for freedom — sometimes getting as high as the limits would allow; sometimes attracted to the big lights which invariably burn them. Others get a sight of freedom, knowing instinctively that there is really life out there to provide them with all they need to live. Yet they haven't found the way out of their trapped and restricted life. Some, like the ladybugs in my loft, never even get to the window to obtain a glimpse of hope, but crawl about on the walls until they finally expire.

For everyone there is life — abundant life — out there. But they're on the inside, looking out! And until they find that one crack in the wall which God has provided — that one door to freedom and life — they're doomed. There is an opening. Listen to what the Apostle John quoted Jesus as saying in John 10:9:

"I am the door. If anyone enters by Me, he will be saved, and will go in and out and find pasture."

So many people are trapped in habits and attempts to find their way to what they hope will be freedom. Sin has them between a hot place and a hard place; like a glass window where they can only get the odd glimpse of what might be. They go for the bright lights and get burned. They look with longing at freedom which is just out of reach. In the very next verse, Jesus explains their position. Look at John 10:10:

"The thief does not come except to steal, and to kill, and to destroy. I have come that they may have life, and that they may have it more abundantly."

Outside, there is freedom and lots to eat. Trapped between the bright lights and the occasional glimpse of what might be, there is nothing but loss, pain, destruction and death. But God loved you so much that He sent Jesus, His only Son, to die for our sins and to open up the only crack; the only door to freedom and abundant life.

Freedom is great, if you can just get it! Back in John 8:36, we read:

"Therefore if the Son makes you free, you shall be free indeed."

Could I invite you to the door to freedom? Let one of our prayer partners show you the way. Call us now (note page 7). There is hope and life out there!

I'M WORKING ON MY UPPER ROOM

In the top of my barn, there is a second storey with a strong board floor, a door out to a deck ten feet off the ground, and a big window at the other end of the barn looking down on the trees and the river. I'm getting it ready as a study and music lounge where I can get away to think, write and study. I call it the "upper room." But it's not quite finished yet. When it's fully prepared, I will enjoy it for the rest of my days. But there's another place even higher up that I'm more excited about....

For several years now, I have been renovating that large upper room in my barn. It is water-proofed and lined with insulation and a vapour barrier. The ceiling has been tiled and walls are up and painted. It still needs a bit more work, but it's slowly getting ready. There's a desk, of course, and enough bookshelves to actually accommodate all my books. And since it is insulated, I have installed a wood stove to heat it.

I used to take about two or three hours a week to work on this big room, and I'm really rather excited about the possibility of actually getting it done completely. I can hardly wait to have it ready and totally done. There's still a lot of trim work to do, even though the furniture is already in. It's my hobby, I guess, and I'm not too bad at carpentry.

I've been looking forward to this place being ready for some time now. There's a lot of work going into it. I can't even smell the livestock downstairs in the egg factory. It will be really nice.

I couldn't help but draw a parallel between my upper room and another place that's being prepared for me. Have you ever read the words of Jesus in John 14:2-3? He says:

"In My Father's house are many mansions; if it were not so, I would have told you. I go to prepare a place for you. And if I go and prepare a place for you, I will come again and receive you to Myself; that where I am, there you may be also."

I have been working on my upper room for about five years, a little at a time. Jesus said these words about 2,000 years ago. And His ability to create is so far beyond my imagination that I can hardly wait to see my new quarters in heaven. Jesus said He's "preparing" a place for you and me. I'm not very sure how God relates time with eternity, but I am sure that when I finally do see heaven and take up permanent residence with the God of the universe, it will be far beyond anything I could dream of. I think He may be just working on the trim; the finishing touches. In fact, in 1 Corinthians 2:9, it is written that:

"Eye has not seen, nor ear heard, nor have entered into the heart of man the things which God has prepared for those who love Him."

And I have to admit, that sounds a lot more exciting than what my upper room in the barn will be like when it's done.

If we consider the signs of Jesus' return, it appears to me that the preparations in heaven by the Lord Himself (for you and me) must nearly be done.

I guess the most important question we can ask ourselves at this stage in world history is: Are we prepared to go to heaven? When

Israel refused to be corrected and reconciled with God, the prophet said in Amos 4:12:

"Therefore thus will I do to you, O Israel; and because I will do this to you, prepare to meet your God, O Israel!"

I think the same warning is for all of us today. We will meet God one day, whether we like the idea or not. And we will either face Him as our judge, or we will face Him as our loving heavenly Father. Jesus, who came to open the gates of heaven to us, said in Luke 12:40:

"Therefore you also be ready, for the Son of Man is coming at an hour you do not expect."

Are you ready? If not, I suggest you get prepared! I'm not suggesting you work on it. Jesus has already done all the work necessary at Calvary. All you need to do to get ready is accept the finished work of God. It's yours forever.

POUNDING A NAIL THROUGH A KNOT

Did you ever try to drive a nail through a knot? I've bent more nails on knots than I care to think about. But after a few attempts, quite often even a knot will take a nail. I had a man write to me some years ago who had a heart like a knot. But after listening to my commentaries for a year — first with anger, then with interest — I finally nailed him. I'll tell you about it.

I know I'm talking about my loft in the barn a lot these days, but bear with me. After all, it did take a lot of time and energy over the last five years to make it what it is today.

Most of the hard work was cleaning the loft and making it fit for human habitation, let alone human noses! A former owner kept his chickens up in an enclosed area in the loft, and they left a definite trail. I have mine isolated into a totally separate area in the lower part of the barn. But now the loft up here, as anyone who visits can see, has changed considerably from the dusty, smelly place it once was.

Our 17-year-old chesterfield, covered with afghans made by Mary's patient hands, provide some comfortable seating, plus odds and ends from various relatives, including a big drum that sits by the window. (My older brother brought it home to Canada on an airline after visiting us in Africa years ago.)

However, prior to achieving this cozy setting in my upper room, I encountered a problem. The rafters were not even, and I had to add shims of various thickness in order to have any semblance of smoothness to the ceiling. To add to the challenge, the original rafters had lots of knots in them.

Did you ever try to drive a nail into a big knot? It's like trying to drive a nail into a block of brass. You bend a lot of nails trying to do so. That's why most people would move to a new spot, and drive a nail where there is no knot. But I'm not your usual person. I can get rather insistent, even about driving a nail. If the knot says NO, I don't readily take no for an answer. You can drive a nail into a knot if you're persistent enough and willing to waste a few nails in the process!

I know some people who are like knots in wood when it comes to hearing and receiving the Gospel of Jesus Christ. They resist the truth with hearts that seem like stone. It seems many a sermon and many a witness has been wasted on them. But if you are persistent and don't mind wasting the first few nails, one of them will finally penetrate. Israel, God's chosen people, were something like my barn loft, and God wanted to clean them up. Listen to how the prophet put it in Ezekiel 36:25-27:

"Then I will sprinkle clean water on you, and you shall be clean; I will cleanse you from all your filthiness and from all your idols. I will give you a new heart and put a new spirit within you; I will take the heart of stone out of your flesh and give you a heart of flesh. I will put My Spirit within you and cause you to walk in My statutes, and you will keep My judgments and do them."

God loves you! And no matter how filthy you've been; no matter how you have been distracted by the idolatrous lifestyles around you; no matter how hard-hearted you have become — God still loves you. He will persist. He has plenty of time and patience. It's you who really doesn't have enough time to waste. God can give you a new heart.

And prayer is part of the process. One year, we emphasized joy on *100 Huntley Street*. The next year, we emphasized strength. Our prayer is much like David's prayer in Psalm 51:12-13:

"Restore to me the joy of Your salvation, and uphold me with Your generous Spirit. Then I will teach transgressors Your ways, and sin-

ners shall be converted to You."

That's why David, Chuck, Jenny, Lorna and I keep pounding away at this nail. We want the truth to penetrate your heart. There are hundreds of people who care about your knot-hard heart, and want the best for you. That's why they pray and help support this ministry. And that's why we'll be back tomorrow, still pounding on the same nail.

We want the truth to penetrate your heart. Why not open up just a crack and let the light start shining in?

Chapter 5

Together We Grow – Apart...
Oh, Brother!

COPY-CATECHISM - Part One

I've been asked many times about some of the different things that seem to happen when revivals take place. Some of the physical manifestations seem to become common in certain areas, churches, or revivals. I can't answer the whole question in this short commentary, but I hope I can give you some basis for thinking it through Scripturally for yourself. God is a God of great diversity. It's we humans who develop habits.

"Birds of a feather flock together," like my chickens. I've got white Leghorns, and I have reddish chickens called Shaver Cross. They were raised separately and differ in age by about three years. When I integrated them a few weeks ago, they seemed to mix well enough. But more often than not, you'll see a group of white hens in one place, and a group of red gals in another.

Now, just as sure as I'm alive, someone is going to jump to the conclusion that I'm going to talk about racism. Well, you're wrong. I'm going to talk about charismatics and Pentecostals.

Most churches have their catechism: a system of study of the doctrines and practices held dear by that particular denomination. And there's nothing wrong with having a catechism.

When I was raised as a Pentecostal, I seemed to have been made to understand that a catechism was not really necessary. As Christians, we should learn to walk in the Spirit and, as individuals, we each need to act and react to the moving of God's Spirit in our own particular way. So we never had a very formalized catechism. But we did have Bible studies, Sunday school and a system of doctrinal studies which, though not always formal, was quite extensive and intense. But the word "catechism" was never used.

The longer I live, the more I believe that in Pentecostal and charismatic circles, we have our own informal catechism. I have coined a phrase to describe it: "copy-catechism"! Let me explain.

We are told in Scripture about the "manifestations of the Spirit" which are, according to 1 Corinthians 12:7-11, as follows:

"But the manifestation of the Spirit is given to each one for the profit of all: for to one is given the word of wisdom through the Spirit, to another the word of knowledge through the same Spirit, to another

faith by the same Spirit, to another gifts of healings by the same
Spirit, to another the working of miracles, to another prophecy, to
another discerning of spirits, to another different kinds of tongues, to
another the interpretation of tongues. But one and the same Spirit
works all these things, distributing to each one individually as He
wills."

We hear of many unusual things happening during revivals. It goes
back beyond the great Pentecostal revival of the turn of the century. It
goes far back beyond the great Methodist revival or the Quakers (who
were so named because of their quaking in the presence of God). It
goes back to the very beginning of the Church: the birthday of the
Church. In the presence of the Holy Spirit, the followers of Christ
were doing what appeared to be bizarre things and the onlookers
came to the assumption that they were drunk.

Human reactions to the presence, glory and power of the Holy
Spirit have varied over the years. But they are all just human reactions
to the powerful presence of God. They are not manifestations of the
Spirit.

I have observed in various places and times, a great variety of
human reactions. Often, such reactions become duplicated in one
place. We are talking about something holy here. This is not a thing to
be either made fun of or to be taken lightly. But we must keep clear in
our understanding that the manifestations of the Spirit are clearly
defined in the Scripture verses we just read. They should (and can) be
clearly taught in a catechism or series of Bible studies.

It is an awesome thing to be in the presence of God, and to sense
His power and majesty. However, sometimes people don't know how
to react, so they simply observe others and copy them. Such human
reactions cannot, and should not, be included in a catechism of study.
Yet they do, inevitably, seem to become a part of a local situation
through copy-catechism.

Some are distracting and disruptive. Others are worshipful and
Christ-honouring. Since we have a choice, let us, as Paul repeats in
Romans 8:1,4:

"...not walk according to the flesh, but according to the Spirit."

Let us neither criticize nor imitate, but let each one of us be sure we are indeed reacting to God by walking in the Spirit as He leads us individually. It's acceptable to quench the flesh, but let us NEVER ever quench the Spirit of God.

COPY-CATECHISM - Part Two

In the previous commentary I mentioned that local habits, even rituals can arise out of local revivals. I called it "copy-catechism." I want to discuss a little more about this whole matter with you, and to advise both openness and caution, for both are essential to stable Christian growth and maturity.

There are various reactions people have to the presence and power of God, and most of us are a little quick to pass judgment. But there are some whom God has chosen, specifically elders, who are mandated to assess the actions, words and deeds of Christians. The principle is reflected in 1 Peter 5:1-2:

"The elders who are among you I exhort...: Shepherd the flock of God which is among you, serving as overseers...."

Some make a career out of expressing their outrage at one thing or another. They can always find something to be against. I'm not talking about them. I'm talking about those who are elders; elders in the local church, as well as recognized elders in the community of churches. These elders should use the Scriptures (all of them in balance) to assess any matter. John 3:6 says:

"That which is born of the flesh is flesh, and that which is born of the Spirit is spirit."

Just as some people pretend to be born-again Christians, others pretend to have a great spiritual experience. Some are in the flesh and some are truly in the Spirit.

Perhaps the most basic assessment of truth, as opposed to error, in every area of Christian experience is defined in 1 John 4:2-3:

"By this you know the Spirit of God: Every spirit that confesses that Jesus Christ has come in the flesh is of God. And every spirit that does not confess that Jesus Christ has come in the flesh is not of God...."

It seems to be much easier to condemn than it is to condone, yet there absolutely MUST be a balance, both Scripturally and rationally, in our understanding of the moving of God's Spirit in both the local church and in any great revival of the Church. Paul sets some of these balanced standards in 1 Thessalonians 5:16-23:

"Rejoice always, pray without ceasing, in everything give thanks; for this is the will of God in Christ Jesus for you. Do not quench the Spirit. Do not despise prophecies. Test all things; hold fast what is good. Abstain from every form of evil. Now may the God of peace Himself sanctify you completely; and may your whole spirit, soul, and body be preserved blameless at the coming of our Lord Jesus Christ."

When local habits develop, and when one copies another's physical reaction when the Spirit of God is upon them, be cautious. *"Test all things,"* Paul said. He also said, *"do not quench the spirit."* It is sometimes a delicate balance, and the decision of the elders may not go down well with some. But to be Scripturally-sound, we must also be Scripturally-obedient.

This "copy-catechism" that has been developed in many areas of revival is probably less harmful than some suppose, but it is also much more distracting than those who do it might assume.

If you want to copy anyone when the Spirit of God comes upon you, judge yourself by the greatest example we could possibly have. Do we measure up, not in physical copy-catechisms, but in the long-lasting ministry for which the Spirit comes? Remember what Jesus read from Isaiah 61:1 about Himself? Let's read it:

"The Spirit of the Lord God is upon Me, because the Lord has anointed Me to preach good tidings to the poor; He has sent Me to heal the brokenhearted, to proclaim liberty to the captives and the opening of the prison to those who are bound."

If the Spirit of God is really upon you, these manifestations will be evident. There will always be those who criticize from inside the Body of Christ, but even more so from outside the Church of Jesus Christ. We read in 1 Peter 4:14:

"If you are reproached for the name of Christ, blessed are you, for the Spirit of glory and of God rests upon you. On their part He is blasphemed, but on your part He is glorified."

When the Spirit of God comes upon you, you may very well exhibit some physical reaction at the altar of a church, but unless you also exhibit a life of holiness and genuine ministry outside the church, you have real reason to question your own integrity.

SPLITTING HAIRS OR WOOD...

Splitting hairs, splitting wood, or splitting churches — that is the question. Splitting wood is necessary for firewood. Splitting hairs can cause tempers to fire up great storms of controversy. And splitting churches through acts of the flesh can cause the fire of God's indignation to blaze. I'd rather split wood for the rest of my life than to cause a church to divide over any issue at all!

One of my more exercise-filled activities back at the barn is splitting wood. It's used for the wood stove right there in the barn, as well as for the fireplace in the house. And there's plenty to split. I have a pile of trees which have been reduced from about 45 or 50 feet high, into a pile of chunks about five or six feet high. The average length is about 12 to 16 inches. There are two reasons why every piece has to be split: 1) it has to fit into the wood stove, and 2) it dries out a lot better when it's split.

Splitting takes a lot of energy. A splitting wedge weighs about six pounds. The axe I use is about four pounds of hard, sharp steel. When I come down on a piece of tree trunk, my intention is clearly to divide it right down the middle. An undivided piece of tree is difficult to burn and heavy to handle. Sometimes a piece is so wet, hard, or knotty that you have to peel slabs off the side, working toward the middle. In any case, when it comes to firewood, splits are necessary.

But splits are not good for churches! Occasionally, a church will be divided over some issue. Often (too often, in fact) it is hair-splitting. And when temperatures rise, a silly hair-splitting issue can quickly grow into a church-splitting tragedy.

The most unfortunate situation is when a person comes into a church as a stranger, slowly makes a position for themselves, and then starts raising issues and looking for supporters in those issues.

Splitting wood is good because it makes the fire burn better and faster. Splitting churches causes the fires of faith and evangelism to burn low and even be snuffed out!

The Bible speaks about the kind of people who cause divisions.

Look at Galatians 5:19-20:

"Now the works of the flesh are evident, which are: adultery, forni-cation, uncleanness, licentiousness [lewdness], idolatry, sorcery, hatred, contentions, jealousies, outbursts of wrath, selfish ambitions, dissensions, heresies...."

These are the works of the flesh! They are all contrary to walking in unity in the Church. Paul says such people should be ostracized in Romans 16:17:

"Now I urge you, brethren, note those who cause divisions and offenses, contrary to the doctrine which you learned, and avoid them."

Avoid them. Stay away from them. They are sharp axes, and they split wherever they strike. When the Church comes together in ser-vice and worship, its members should come in unity of mind and pur-pose. Paul had to address a problem once in 1 Corinthians 11:18-19:

"For first of all, when you come together as a church, I hear that there are divisions among you, and in part I believe it. For there must also be factions among you, that those who are approved may be rec-ognized among you."

That statement seems strange: *"...there must be factions among you...."* Yet, it is so. For when a faction acts in the flesh, whether in heresy, morality or simple hair-splitting doctrinal arguments, those who are in the flesh will eventually be recognized and find them-selves on the outside. The Church of Jesus Christ is to be a self-purify-ing Body, indwelt by the Holy (I repeat, HOLY) Spirit of God.

In 1 Corinthians 1:10, Paul pleads for unity.

"Now I plead with you, brethren, by the name of our Lord Jesus Christ, that you all speak the same thing, and that there be no divi-sions among you, but that you be perfectly joined together in the same mind and in the same judgment."

Unconfessed or hidden immorality can divide a church. Heresy and doctrinal hair-splitting can divide a church just as surely as an axe splits wood. The only difference is that a piece of wood is meant to be burned. Those who split churches are not meant to be burned, but they will face the fire of God's indignation. The judgment seat of Christ is a very real event in God's calendar for the future! I wouldn't want to face God, having caused a church to split!

HOT OR COLD

Several of us as leaders of the Crossroads Ministry met for prayer and discussion in the nice, warm, comfortable loft of my barn. We really only had one disagreement. It was over the temperature in the barn. I thought 72 degrees Fahrenheit was quite adequate. However, some of the others were not comfortable until it was 85 degrees.

When you go to church, is the temperature to your satisfaction? How hot should we let the church get? Can everyone really be satisfied in the church? An interesting question....

This amusing incident happened one week last winter. Several of us who are leaders here at the Crossroads Centre were meeting in my loft in the upper part of my barn. It was a frigid day and, of course, meeting in a barn for a planning and discussion session doesn't seem like a very natural thing to do. And, on top of that, who ever heard of a barn that was warm?

When these men, including our doctor of psychology, Chuck Borsellino, came trooping into my loft, their expectations were that it would be cold. Leather jackets and sweaters were in abundance. Even though I had three heaters and stoves going and the loft is totally insulated, they expected to be cold! I will admit, it had only reached 68 degrees Fahrenheit when they arrived. But within a little while, it had reached the comfortable 72 degrees. So, I switched off one of the heaters.

Immediately there was a chorus of objections: "It's cold in here!" "Why did you turn off the heat, it's too cold?" Well, being the nice fellow I am, I turned the heater back on. And the heat climbed to 80 degrees. So I turned off the heat a second time. Again, objections with Dr. Chuck leading the pack! So I turned the heat back on. Well, with both heaters going, it soon reached 85 degrees. This time, I drew their attention to the thermometer, pointing out that it was 85 degrees. They were still cold. "There's something wrong with the thermometer," they said. In consideration of my guests, I only turned it down a bit. Well, it maintained a very warm temperature of 85 degrees.

Finally, several of them started peeling off their layers of sweaters, saying nothing. I grinned to myself, then asked them why they were taking off their sweaters. "It's too hot in here now," they sheepishly said. I turned off the heater. With one heater, the temperature slowly went down to about 74 degrees and this time no one was uncomfortable.

Here is my interpretation of the situation. Except for David Mainse and myself, none of the others were psychologically prepared to be warm in what they thought had to be a "cold" barn — including the head of our counselling centre, Dr. Chuck Borsellino. In fact, I'm going to offer him some counselling!

It's sometimes like this in a church. This is not to do with the degrees on the thermometer, but more to do with the "spiritual" temperature of the church. People sometimes feel their church is cold, and they begin praying for revival. As people do that earnestly and honestly, the church will begin to change; the spiritual temperature will rise. People, who think they own the church (like I own my barn) and think it's hot enough, will try to turn down the heat. But others want more warmth. They want a real hot revival. Then when real revival does come to the church, they start getting uncomfortable, so they fidget and distance themselves from the fire. They say, "A normal warm spiritual temperature is fine. Let's not get too hot here. We don't want to be called fanatics!"

I must admit, when my barn gets to 85 degrees, that's too hot for me. But when a church has revival, I love it. Jesus made a statement about the spiritual temperature of His followers when he spoke to the church in Laodicea in Revelation 3:15-16:

"I know your works, that you are neither cold nor hot. I could wish you were cold or hot. So then, because you are lukewarm, and neither cold nor hot, I will spew [vomit] you out of My mouth."

Jesus spoke of this in another way to His disciples in Matthew 12:30 when He explained that a house divided against itself will fall:

"He who is not with Me is against Me, and he who does not gather with Me scatters abroad."

So, go ahead. Let the heat rise. But do it in full unity of the Spirit and you will see revival in your church.

By the way, when we left my loft in the barn, we were in full unity in our thinking and prayerful planning for the future of this ministry. And the temperature was HOT!

DID YOU EVER WATCH A FLOWER GROW?

Isn't spring a great time of year? Flowers come out of the ground. They are unrecognizable when they first squeeze out of the cold earth; but when they are in full bloom, what an infinite variety: roses, peonies, daffodils, crocuses, tulips, dandelions, daisies and snapdragons — all in the same garden. All we can take the credit for is *where* they are, not *what* they are. I'm quite happy that life itself doesn't depend on me. I just plant seeds.

Every year I am fascinated when spring suddenly brings nature into life again. Little green things come out of the ground. The grass becomes lush and, quite frankly, annoyingly thick and difficult to mow. It often jams my lawn mower at this time of year.

What really gets my attention is those little green and sometimes almost white things that sprout out of the flower gardens. Sometimes they're reddish or even yellowish. And sometimes you're not even sure at first what breed of flower they might be, even though you planted them yourself. Then, within days, they take on a shape and colour of their own, and you begin to recognize crocuses, tulips, daffodils, peonies and, of course, weeds. There are always a few weeds which sneak in there no matter how carefully you try to keep them out. That's the best time to get rid of them, by the way: when they first appear and before their roots get too deep.

The day then comes when a little bud appears on a stem. It slowly inches its way higher and higher as its leaves grow with it to protect its own little private territory. Fascinating! Then there is the day the bud begins to open. Eventually it fully opens and you can see all the beauty of colour, shape and form, with its detailed veins and velvety purity — all because someone planted a seed or a bulb. It may have been planted a year or even two before. During the winter, it lay dormant for a long time, enduring cold and harshness, until the sun drew life to the surface so the full bloom could take place.

Have you ever planted a seed or a bulb? If you have, you know what I'm talking about. But you also know that you were simply limited to the planting of the seed. You didn't make it grow, even though you may have provided some water and fertilizer. It was God who made the flower so intricately that it would respond to warmth and water, and grow into something so beautiful.

If you have planted a spiritual seed or bulb, have you ever watched it grow? This is even more thrilling than the eventual blooming of a flower. And you didn't make *that* grow either. God did. It's a little dangerous to take the credit for something God does, even though He may have used you as a planter. Look at what the Word of God says in 1 Corinthians 3:7:

"So then neither he who plants is anything, nor he who waters, but God who gives the increase."

Even Job, many thousands of years ago, recognized this basic principle and asked his unfriendly friends (who thought they were friends) a very pointed question. It is in Job 38:25-27:

"Who has divided a channel for the overflowing water, or a path for the thunderbolt, to cause it to rain on a land where there is no one, a wilderness in which there is no man; to satisfy the desolate waste, and cause to spring forth the growth of tender grass?"

God always uses people, including gifted people. And let's not make the all too common mistake that these people are ordained ministers filling pulpits. They can also be found in the pew, and in the spiritual gardens of the world. Look at Ephesians 4:11-12:

"And He Himself gave some to be apostles, some prophets, some evangelists, and some pastors and teachers, for the equipping of the saints for the work of ministry, for the edifying of the Body of Christ."

Did you get that? *"...for the equipping of the SAINTS for the work of the ministry"!*

A sower went forth to sow! Was that you? If not, you'll never ever enjoy the birth and growth of a beautiful new flower in God's garden. You may not recognize, at first, what kind it might be or what denomination, but that doesn't matter. The garden is God's anyway!

I speak of Christ and His Church, of course! This is the perfect time for planting with the seed of the Word of God. It always is!

OUTSIDE, LOOKING IN

Part of my loft used to be a birdhouse for pigeons. It must have been heaven to those pigeons. Now I have birds sitting on the windowsills looking in. But I also have set up birdhouses all over the place. Some are for sparrows, others for bluebirds, and also some for smaller types. I like birds, no matter what kind they are. And, I like Christians too, no matter what denomination they are. After all, we're all going to the same heaven (as long as our names are registered in the right place).

I have a very small window looking out over a creek which runs past the back of my property. It's just to the right of my desk up in the "upper room" where I read, study, pray and write these commentaries. The window used to be a part of the house. The two sealed panes of glass began to leak and become foggy, so I had to put a new one in the house. I used the old one to build a little window over a spot where there used to be an entrance to the old pigeon loft in the barn. Now it's weatherproof and tight. But there is still a small ledge where birds often come and sit, sometimes looking in at me as I write.

I try to behave myself, making sure I don't respond with fast movements, so I can watch them for a while. Yet, as soon as I do something sudden that disturbs them, they get frightened and fly away. But they often come back for another look. Some are becoming almost fearless because they realize my movements have never caused them harm. They just sit on the outside, looking in!

I've decided to build a little birdhouse just at the edge of the window on the outside to offer them a home; a place to nest and raise their young. Every bird needs a home. Actually I've decided to make the birdhouse in the shape and appearance of a church.

I'm not sure what goes through the little bird's brain as it stares in the window, but perhaps it looks like heaven to them: warm, protected from the wind and rain; a haven with lots of room and even shelter when the sun is too hot. Who knows what a bird thinks, or even if it does think? But I'm sure this little church-shaped birdhouse will be a sanctuary from the harshness of life, at least for as long as this life remains.

I've got a dozen or more birdhouses around the property. One is a duplex. Several have been painted and decorated by my wife Mary. Different kinds of birds use different kinds of birdhouses. Some birds just don't bother. They would rather live in the trees. They're on the outside looking in from a distance.

I think of all these little birdhouses as churches of various denominations for different kinds of birds and their needs. They are *all* used, but some people remain on the outside, just watching; looking in from a distance. Some would like to get in only to steal eggs or the young hatchlings. However, some actually go into the church and take up residence for life. They have found a safe sanctuary where there is more protection than living out in the wilds and in the fast lane. Churches should always provide a safe sanctuary from the storms of life.

Some birdhouses we've bought, others I've built. But the big one, the final sanctuary where the whole flock of God will reside, is being built by God. Listen to Jesus in Matthew 16:18:

"...I will build My church, and the gates of Hades shall not prevail against it."

Now, I have no idea which birdhouse, excuse me, denomination, to which you belong. But, quite frankly, it doesn't concern me too much. What concerns me is not that your name is registered in the local church, but in heaven. We're talking about relationship here, not membership in a birdhouse. Listen to Hebrews 12:22-23:

"But you have come to Mount Zion and to the city of the living God, the heavenly Jerusalem, to an innumerable company of angels, to the general assembly and church of the firstborn who are registered in heaven, to God the Judge of all, to the spirits of just men made perfect."

There are no perfect birdhouses or denominations, but there can be perfected Christians through that personal relationship with God. Look at 2 Corinthians 5:17:

"...if anyone is in Christ, he is a new creation; old things have passed away; behold, all things have become new."

This can only be achieved *in* Christ. Not on the outside looking in! It's the perfect solution to your life's problems. Come on in! Don't stay on the outside looking in!

SO, I'M DIGGING A HOLE

I'm digging a pond for goldfish in my back yard. It's a back-breaking job. At this point, it's a very strictly denominational pond: goldfish only. Later on, I might try to include a few other kinds of fish, but I sure don't want them trying to bite and devour one another. So, for now, goldfish only. It would be nice if all fish got along well, but that's just not the way it is at the moment. Something like denominations, don't you think?

For the past several years, we have had a half-wooden barrel in our back yard where we kept a few goldfish. Their beautiful fantails and leisurely, well-fed life appealed to me. I wouldn't mind it myself, except that it's under water, and I can't breathe too well under those circumstances.

The first year we had the goldfish (just before the weather began to freeze), we released them into a neighbour's large pond (with his permission, of course). They are still there and have grown rather large. But then, the cold weather set in so quickly that it froze the top of the water. We hoped they'd survive, but the weather was more severe than usual in our neck of the woods. When the thaw finally came, it was all over for them. I couldn't even find a little bone. It's my fault. I should have let them join their relatives in the larger pond which doesn't freeze all the way to the bottom.

So, I'm hand-digging a little pond that will be deep enough for their survival in the winter months. I'm getting pains in some muscles I forgot I even owned. But I am providing a more comfortable and lasting home for my little denomination of fish. People, just like fish, need a safe place when the tough times suddenly come. Look at Ecclesiastes 9:12:

"For man also does not know his time: like fish taken in a cruel net, like birds caught in a snare, so the sons of men are snared in an evil time, when it falls suddenly upon them."

That's why we have churches. Even though there are many denominations of churches, there is really only one Church of the Lord Jesus Christ. That's the Church Jesus said He would build. That's the final destiny of all those who are brought in by God's fishermen within the safety net of the Gospel of Jesus Christ.

When Jesus was calling His disciples into scholarships under His teaching, He revealed to them right off the top what their eventual responsibilities would be. Look at what He said to some of them when He found them cleaning their own fishing nets, in Matthew 4:19:

"And He said to them, "Follow Me, and I will make you fishers of men."

Fishers of men! Quite a concept. And when an evangelist — a fisher of men — goes into the troubled waters of the world, he must be careful when he draws in the net. If roughly treated, a fish might die before it's time. And it's the same with the souls of men: if roughly treated, they may die before their time. A true soul-winner must be gentle, as gentle as he would be on himself; in fact, just as gently as Jesus cares for the Church. Look at Ephesians 5:29:

"For no one ever hated his own flesh, but nourishes and cherishes it, just as the Lord does the church."

There are various ponds in which fish live at the moment. And there are a variety of denominations in which God's schools of fish abide at the moment. But one day, all the denominations of this world will give way to the final gathering of the saints into the universal gathering of the whole Body of Christ Jesus our Lord. Paul described it back in Ephesians 4:4-6:

"There is one body and one Spirit, just as you were called in one hope of your calling; one Lord, one faith, one baptism; one God and Father of all, who is above all, and through all, and in you all."

Yes, we have our own denominations, but there is but one Saviour! Yes, we have our own schools of thought, but there is One Final Truth and that is found in Jesus Christ, not just in your pond.

Someday, in God's great heaven, we will all be gathered together in one great Body. That's why it's a good idea to keep from messing around in someone else's pond, and keep fishing in the rest of God's needy world! It's not your denominational distinctive which saves you. It's faith in Jesus Christ!

FALLOW GROUND

I don't like an unproductive garden plot. Lying fallow for a year is alright, but when it goes on too long, it can become a place for the growth of the wrong stuff, like weeds. If left too long, it becomes very hard and very difficult to work. Seeds sown on it will be stolen by birds, and what does take root grows poorly because the roots can't get the amount of air they need. Fallow ground becomes useless. Have you been lying fallow for too long?

I was struck with a thought. Have you ever really been *struck* with a thought? It was as sudden and as effective as a good solid slap on the head.

Fallow ground! That is a former field or garden which at one time was productive, but has been lying unused for a period of time. During that fallow period, the soil gets a rest, and nutrients and natural fertilizers are refreshed in that soil by falling rain, snow and even certain living things like birds and earthworms.

But it is fallow; lying unused and unproductive. It's good to let land rest to be refreshed, refurbished and fertilized. In fact, that's an ancient concept that still has great merit. But lying fallow can go on too long. It could well revert to wild overgrowth, and become nothing but weeds, brush and hard earth.

I had just such a piece of garden. When I put the Rototiller into it, chopping and spinning into this fallow ground, I noticed a few things. The stones which were in the soil had been pushed to the surface by the frost. I threw them aside. But the soil had become hard and, of course, unreceptive to seeding.

I couldn't help but think of some Christians who have lain fallow for too long. They have become hard, unproductive and unreceptive to God's Word, which is the Seed. Stones have appeared and weeds have even begun to grow. Oh, the soil is still good, but it needs to be worked again. It needs to be broken and loosened up, so that air can get into it in order for valuable things to grow once again.

The Church of Jesus Christ in many places has become fallow ground for too long. We have become less productive. We have become hard, with stones and weeds infesting and retarding the purpose of God. It is not too different from the time when God sent the prophet Jeremiah to call them to repentance; a return to seeking after God and righteousness. Look at Jeremiah 4:1-3:

"'If you will return, O Israel,' says the Lord, 'return to Me; and if

*you will put away your abominations out of My sight, then you shall
not be moved. And you shall swear, The Lord lives, in truth, in judgment, and in righteousness; the nations shall bless themselves in
Him, and in Him they shall glory.' For thus says the Lord to the men
of Judah and Jerusalem: 'Break up your fallow ground, and do not sow
among thorns.'"*

Many people are seeking God for revival in the Church, and God is
blessing in some places. We praise God for that. But the Church is in
need of a stirring up; a breaking up of the fallow ground to allow the
wind of the Spirit to move through and produce more and greater
fruit.

This is not always a comfortable experience. A Rototiller hits hard
with its tangs, and breaks into smaller pieces what have become hard
lumps. It takes more than one pass of the tiller to make the soil receptive to seed, air and the breath of life once again. Weeds and stones
are not always easy to get out, but they MUST come out.

Just so, in our lives individually as Christians, and together as the
Church, we need to break up our fallow ground, get rid of the shallow, and go a bit deeper. Get rid of injustice, unrighteousness and
church politics, and become receptive to God's righteousness and His
Seed, which is the Word of God. The prophet Hosea repeated the
same type of message in Hosea 10:12:

*"Sow for yourselves righteousness; reap in mercy; break up your fal-
low ground, for it is time to seek the Lord, till He comes and rains
righteousness on you."*

Let's not continue to lay fallow! Let's break up our fallow ground —
our hearts and souls — and seek God for a visitation of His Spirit, so
that in these last days we may see the greatest harvest ever.

Break up your fallow ground!

GROWING AT GROUND LEVEL

Some things grow up and other things grow across. My garden has
been full of both. But one thing is absolutely essential: they all need
roots. My pumpkins have grown faster than some churches. In fact,
they grew faster than some Christians as well. Why? Roots. Just plain
and simple, strong and healthy roots.

One fall, when I was cleaning out my gardens, getting ready to till the ground in preparation for the next year's crop, I noticed something rather interesting. In one garden, I had raspberries at one end, strawberries at the other, and several rows of onions and pumpkins in the large central part. Before I could till the soil, I had to get the pumpkin vines out of the way so they would not wind around the tangs of my tiller and cause it to seize up.

The first thing I noticed was that the larger pumpkins on the vine were those closest to the original root I had planted. The further from the root the other pumpkins on the same vine were, the smaller the size. The second thing I noticed was that the vines had established secondary roots at fairly regular distances from the original plant. They were able to supply supplementary nourishment to the vine, and to the other pumpkins further down the vine.

These vines spread in every direction from the original plant. When I tried to reroute them, it most often retarded their growth. Some of the shoots from the main plant headed out across the lawn. These shoots produced very small pumpkins. Since the grass held them too high from the soil, they could not send down secondary roots.

I saw a parallel in the establishment of a "mother" church, with branch churches growing in various directions from it. The original plant produced the largest pumpkin nearby. However, the further the other pumpkins were from the original plant, the less nourishment they were able to receive from the main root. Churches grow the same way. Or, they should!

On the other hand, I have seen some folk plant pumpkins in a different manner. When the first real pumpkin appears and starts growing, they cut off all the other flowers before they can produce additional pumpkins (although they may let some secondary roots take hold). The result is a single, massive pumpkin that may win a prize, but one that is too big to really be useful for anything else. In other words, it's too big to handle!

Now, I am not against there being very large churches. On the other hand, I see the Scriptural pattern of church planting. New churches must come from a mother church. They have to have roots somewhere before they can put down roots of their own. They need to be responsible to a mother church until they become self-sustaining with sufficient roots for themselves in good soil.

One pumpkin which had begun to grow on the lawn around my garden had been successful in putting down some secondary roots. However, it was cut off (accidentally, in this case) from the mother vine and eventually shrivelled and died. The soil had not been prepared and its roots had not gone down far enough to be established. Independence can be a dangerous thing. Look at Jesus' parable of the sower in Matthew 13:6:

"But when the sun was up they were scorched, and because they had no root they withered away."

If your roots are not deep down, where there's nourishment and water, you can wither and die spiritually. And we can't compare ourselves to others by what we see on the surface. We rarely know the true roots of another branch of the vine, even though we may be a branch of the same vine. In Romans 11:18, we read:

"...do not boast against the branches. But if you do boast, remember that you do not support the root, but the root supports you."

Churches consisting of groups of Christians, as well as individual Christians, should avoid what might be called supplementary aids to Christian growth. I'm talking about splits over personalities, church politics and sometimes downright deceptions. These things are wicked. Look at Proverbs 12:3:

"A man is not established by wickedness, but the root of the righteous cannot be moved."

If the need for roots in good topsoil is essential to the growth of mere pumpkins, how much more are roots that are well-established in God's Word and strongly attached to the vine important to every Christian.

I MADE SOME GREAT TURKEY SOUP!

I'm not the best cook in the world, but I'm not the worst either! At least that's what I'm told by my own taste buds. I made turkey soup to die for. Actually, it was a turkey who died for the soup! Well, somebody had to do it! But, oh the aroma that filled the house when I was making that soup. I think I put things in that soup that no one would ever have thought of.... And, no, I don't have a recipe for this one, but you can read on if you like.

I must admit that Mary's the best cook in the family. But, just after Thanksgiving, I got it in my head one evening that I'd take all the bones and some of the meat from the Thanksgiving turkey, and make turkey soup. I've never done it before.

Mary was sick in bed and, not being the kind of guy that wastes good food, I thought I'd take my own personal crack at making soup. My father used to have a saying that came out of the depression: "Better to bust your belly than to waste food!" A kind of "eat when it's available" philosophy.

Now, once again, it was Mary's recipe (stored in her head, of course) that formed the basis of this soup. I say "basis" for a reason. I got the basis from Mary, but I had a few ideas of my own. So, I boiled the bones for what seemed like forever, drained off the broth, picked the meat off the bones (with clean hands and a pure heart), put it in the fridge, then went to bed.

The next evening, I started in on phase two. I cut up some potatoes, carrots, threw in some spices, and boiled away. Later, I added a few peas. That was Mary's approach. Then I thought of a few ideas of my own. Like, why not add some corn and barley? Well, we didn't have barley, so I threw in some rice. I ended up with enough soup that, a month later, we were still eating and loving it. (Well, my daughter Elaine didn't like it too much as she's not a big fan of pepper!) We had so much soup, that I froze it in quart and half-quart sealing jars. I'm going to do it again at Christmas, if we can find a willing turkey!

This makes me think of the Church. Not that it's made up of a bunch of turkeys — useless scraps of bones until we get into God's recipe. (Although, if we're honest, most of us are a bunch of turkeys most of the time!)

You see, the Church is made up of all kinds of ingredients, or people. Some of us were just plain turkeys before we got in with the right crowd. Then, there are those who add spice; and others, like potatoes, who add strength and body to the Church. A few are like carrots, which add colour and flavour; and celery sticks which seem rather soft and watery at first, but add that special little taste to the whole. Then there are those who are the salt of the earth and, much to some people's chagrin, there are those who are as hot as pepper. When we put them all together, we get a great Church — a Church with variety, colour, flavour and life! When every person in the Church (no matter their personal differences) is totally integrated like soup, the aroma smells good to God. Look at Ephesians 5:2:

"And walk in love, as Christ also has loved us and given Himself for us, an offering and a sacrifice to God for a sweet-smelling aroma."

Some, like the bones of a turkey, may be rejected by others. Yet, in the whole mix of the Church, they are really the chosen basics. Look at 1 Peter 2:4-5:

"Coming to Him as to a living stone, rejected indeed by men, but chosen by God and precious, you also, as living stones, are being built up a spiritual house, a holy priesthood, to offer up spiritual sacrifices acceptable to God through Jesus Christ."

You see, the Church of Jesus Christ is the only real mixing pot that brings people of various ethnic, educational, racial and religious backgrounds together in harmony. Paul states the following in Galatians 3:28:

"There is neither Jew nor Greek, there is neither slave nor free, there is neither male nor female; for you are all one in Christ Jesus."

Just as I made the "almost" perfect soup (I say this with a little exaggeration), God is building His Church. And every time He adds a new ingredient, it gets better and better!

By the way, are you in yet? The Church, I mean!

JOY COMES IN THE MORNING

My chickens are very kind to me, and entertaining, and productive too. All my chickens laid eggs yesterday. If it wasn't for those eggs, I wouldn't bother having chickens. One of the most interesting times of the day is when I am in the loft, writing commentaries before daylight, and the henhouse comes to life. Within minutes of daybreak, there are all kinds of sounds, thumps and squawking which can only be interpreted as great rejoicing. Morning is a great time in a chicken coop.

While I'm writing commentaries in the loft of my barn, I usually start before daylight. As the sun begins to rise, I can hear the chickens start moving off their roosts, heading for the feed troughs and water. A general stir begins as soon as daylight begins to come in through the windows.

Some of my birds, when they fly down off their roosts, crash land into a wall, and end up in a pile of legs, wings and feathers on the floor. It doesn't seem to hurt them. They get up, shake themselves, and start their day. Within a few minutes of the beginning of their day, I hear a regular thump... thump... thump.... Six in all. Then there are another six thumps. And still another set of thumps. (You have to know my chicken coop to know what is going on.)

During these series of thumps, which go on until about noon, there are anywhere from 25 to 30 communal times of rejoicing. One chicken will start the chorus, and most of the rest will join in. This is what actually happens. They roost as high as they can get on the poles I have mounted near the ceiling of the coop for two reasons: 1) it's warmer up there; and 2) their instincts tell them that if there is a predator around, it will go for the chicken at the lowest level. There's a certain amount of fear and caution at night.

During their sleep, their bodies build big, brown, beautiful eggs. It's quite a natural process. When the sun rises, they leave caution to the winds, fly into the walls, crash land, shake themselves, then eat, drink and be merry. The thump... thump... thump... process is the sound of the chickens jumping up a ladder-like affair I have built so they can get to the nests where they lay their eggs. When a hen lays an egg, she breaks out in rejoicing that she has successfully produced, and the rest of the coop joins in the rejoicing. Satisfied clucking goes on all day as they scratch, eat, drink and prepare for the next vigilant night, and the next jubilant morning.

All this happens because someone benevolent is in overall charge of the whole coop, providing food, shelter and protection: ME! It's much like the people under the rule of King Solomon. In 1 Kings 4:20, we read:

"Judah and Israel were as numerous as the sand by the sea in multitude, eating and drinking and rejoicing."

Once in a while, I'm peeved by the stupidity of my chickens. But I don't separate a chicken from its head just because they get underfoot too often. I'm more interested in the morning, when the eggs come and the rejoicing begins. In Psalm 30:5, we read about God's example of this:

"For His anger is but for a moment, His favour is for life; Weeping may endure for a night, but joy comes in the morning."

My biggest concern is that they get along together, without too much hen-pecking and squabbling among themselves. I want them to rejoice at the fruit of their labours. And that's simply because I benefit too. This is just like the way God looks at His Church. Let's read Romans 12:10-13:

"Be kindly affectionate to one another with brotherly love, in honour giving preference to one another; not lagging in diligence, fervent in spirit, serving the Lord; rejoicing in hope, patient in tribulation, continuing steadfastly in prayer; distributing to the needs of the saints, given to hospitality."

It's a healthy chicken coop that produces eggs. And it's a healthy Church that produces fruit, even though it may be a somewhat painful procedure at times. Look at Psalm 126:6:

"He who continually goes forth weeping, bearing seed for sowing, shall doubtless come again with rejoicing, bringing his sheaves with him."

Now read 1 Thessalonians 2:19 with me:

"For what is our hope, or joy, or crown of rejoicing? Is it not even you in the presence of our Lord Jesus Christ at His coming?"

Paul's great joy came in producing fruit: those who followed and believed in Jesus Christ. Eggs break, but souls are saved for eternity.

I guess the question is: Are you just roosting, or are you producing?

Chapter 6

Groceries, Green Fields and Worm Wars

THE ULTIMATE IN SELFISHNESS

Last summer I read something in the newspapers about "worm wars." Groups of people, who picked dew worms for selling to fishermen, were competing for places to pick worms. The violence escalated until some pretty awful incidents took place. This included running cars off the roads which caused some serious injuries. I've really never thought worms were worth fighting over, but I saw it first hand right in my own back yard the other day. Is a worm worth dying for? I think not!

I guess I've seen an example of the ultimate in selfishness. It happened out at the barn, of course. It happened at one of my "recesses."

When I'm writing a commentary, I usually sit down and write two, one after the other. Then I take a recess. I do something to rest the old brain; something that diverts my attention from concentrated writing. As it happened, this diversion was after a rain, and the chickens had not yet been let out into their runway. So, I chose to do that as my diversion.

As I opened the door, all the old faithful hens raced toward the door in anticipation. I stood at the door as they gingerly darted past me into the freedom of the yard.

As many of you who have any interest in fishing know, dew worms come up for a breather after a night rain, and at dawn they are particularly catchable. One of these crawlers-of-the-night made the mistake of coming up, and staying up, right in the middle of the chicken run. One sharp-eyed old hen saw it and made a beeline for a chicken's equivalent of bacon and eggs. She got it by one end, and gave it a shake. Unfortunately, every other hen in the yard wanted to eat off her plate. It was every hen for herself. Darting and dodging, she raced around the yard with this dew worm flapping around her ears as she ran. Finally, in desperation, she flew past me and back into the henhouse.

What she didn't count on was another hen on her way out, after dutifully laying my breakfast for the next morning. Slam! A head-on collision. She not only lost her worm, but her balance as well. When the two chickens got back to their feet, they looked around in confusion. The worm had disappeared! Why was I not surprised?

This whole affair seemed rife with selfishness, greediness and com-petition. And it didn't even have to happen. There were other tasty worms out in the yard, and they all could have had some. But no, they had to have the one the other hen had. Chickens aren't that much dif-ferent from children in that respect. With five children and twenty-five toys, they sometimes all want the same one.

Let's face it. We adults aren't that much different. We just happen to be more sophisticated, clever and even sneaky in how we go about it. And, of course, modern advertising capitalizes on that fact. They are enticing us all not to just keep up with the Jones', but to pass them at high speed in a new, better, more beautiful car; or microwave; or weed killer for your lawn; or even a better hair implant for receding heads. Yes, I said "heads," not "hairlines." For that's where it all begins: in the head. We have been so confused by mar-keters that we don't even know what we want, let alone what we need. As long as we get the better of the next guy.

Well, good old Solomon had something to say about that. Look at Proverbs 15:27:

"He who is greedy for gain troubles his own house, but he who hates bribes will live."

Sneaky corporate stealing is just as rotten as purse-snatching. Bribery eventually causes you to crash into the next chicken, lose your gains as well as your balance, and maybe even your life. Look at Proverbs 1:19:

"So are the ways of everyone who is greedy for gain; it takes away the life of its owners."

Solomon had a lot to say about this. He recommended a more last-ing commodity than just things, or worms (or "takataka" which means "junk" in Swahili). Look at Proverbs 3:13-14:

"Happy is the man who finds wisdom, and the man who gains understanding; for her proceeds are better than the profits of silver, and her gain than fine gold."

The Apostle Paul wrapped up this truth in one short phrase, in 1 Timothy 6:6:

"Now godliness with contentment is great gain."

So don't waste your time on worms. Worms rot! Go for something you can take with you!

YOU HAVE TO BE READY!

Did you ever go through the grocery store and when you got to the checkout, you reached for your wallet to find it was at home on your dresser? Bad feeling! When you go shopping, you have to be prepared. Well, when we got a couple of goats a while back, we had to be prepared too. You simply have to be ready when you plan for the future. And your wallet will inevitably be involved. Our goats cost something, but now they are paying off — big time!

My little farm is growing! I don't mean it is growing in acreage, but it's growing in productivity. As most of you already know, I have chickens. I've had chickens almost since the first few months we moved onto our little three-and-a-half acre place in the country. We have also had ducks. All my ducks went into the ministry. I'm a minister, and I'm the ministry into which the ducks went.

A while ago, we, or I should say, my wife and daughter, decided we should have a couple of goats. At first I wasn't too excited about this since I've smelled goats before. But when they told me they were twin ewes, and that they were Angora goats which produce mohair for beautiful soft sweaters, I decided to say yes. I can go along with that decision especially if I get a beautiful soft sweater out of it!

So, our little farm operation was about to expand in productivity. But to expand for this productivity, we had to get ready. We had to build a fence strong enough so the goats could not break through. That cost a few dollars. Then, of course, we had to convert the old henhouse into a goat house. That cost a bit too. And we had to get hay to feed them for the winter and some grain to supplement their feed. We were getting ready to expand our little operation so we would be prepared for the future.

Well, I'm happy to tell you that all these preparations have paid off, and we already have a big sack stuffed full of that precious, soft, furry hair that will one day be a beautiful, glistening, soft sweater. I'm made to understand that this particular hair is a very valuable type of wool or yarn. It's been worth all the expense and preparation. We've already had a little sample carded and spun. It's really soft; angora soft.

The Crossroads Ministry is doing much the same thing right now.

We have been instructed by the board of directors to apply for a twenty-four hour license for the Burlington area to more effectively reach this area with "Life-Changing Television." Production plans are already in place. And when we speak of productivity here at *100 Huntley Street*, we are not speaking only of increased programming, but a vastly increased response on our telephones from people who are seeking God, seeking peace, and seeking salvation in the chaotic and despotic society in which we live. Our end product is not just programs. It is precious souls brought into a relationship with God through Jesus Christ, the Son of the Living God.

However, these preparations cost something. No, we have not increased the size of our building. In fact, our staff has actually been reduced in size. We are not going to build more buildings. We are simply going to be more efficient in the use of what we have, in both facilities and people. The extra costs will primarily be for the "ministry" aspects of *100 Huntley Street*.

As vice president of missions, I am asking that you support this ministry as we move into increased productivity and ministry in the future. Now, some people have a problem when someone asks for financial support. But it is a very Biblical concept. In fact, in the days of King Hezekiah, he didn't ask, he commanded! Look at 2 Chronicles 31:4:

"Moreover he commanded the people who dwelt in Jerusalem to contribute support for the priests and the Levites, that they might devote themselves to the Law of the Lord."

The priests and Levites were the ministers of God to His people. Of course, we're not commanding, but we are asking. We're not asking for ourselves, but for the multitudes who are in confusion in our country. The prophet said in Joel 3:14:

"Multitudes, multitudes in the valley of decision! For the day of the Lord is near in the valley of decision."

Television can reach the multitudes. The address to which you can contribute support is in the back of this book. Please write or phone right now and make a pledge of your support for the growing productivity and ministry of *100 Huntley Street*!

You may not get a glistening white mohair sweater out of it, but you

WILL lay up for yourself treasures in heaven! Your investment will pay off — big time!

FAR FIELDS ARE GREENER?

We live in a world of amazing opportunities. Too many, in fact! It seems that most people want more and better than they have. Very few people in this age of abundance are really content. Things that are just out of reach are more attractive than the familiar and the tried and true. Are there no boundaries in human behaviour and human desire any more? Should we all chase after the better, the bigger, the distant greener fields?

I remember a small prayer meeting here at Crossroads. Rev. Bob Scrivens was speaking, and he touched on a thought that I had some long time ago, but forgot. He described a large grazing area for cattle, divided into four quarters. In each quarter was one cow. Every one of the four had her head pushed through the fence and was feeding on the grass on the other side of the fence. Far away fields look greener!

I had seen the same thing any number of times with my chickens. If they were within their compound, they would be running up and down the fence, looking for a way through to the grass on the other side. If they did happen to get out, they would then spend their time running up and down the fence looking for a way in.

My goats, or I should say, my daughter's goats, are enclosed in a large area with plenty of greens to eat. Yet, when I walk into their enclosure with weeds in my hand, they will come and with enthusiasm eat my weeds, even though they are exactly the same as the weeds growing in their grazing area. In fact, they almost climb the fence to get at what appears to be something better on the other side of the fence. It's really remarkable since the weeds are the same, inside and out.

What is even more remarkable is that we humans have the same trait as cows, chickens and goats. We want what we see on the other side of the fence. It looks greener, it seems more attractive, and who needs boundaries anyway?

People without God dislike the boundaries God puts on them. Potiphar's wife was one of these people. She had a husband of her own, yet she looked across the fence at Joseph, her husband's slave in Egypt. Look at Genesis 39:7:

"And it came to pass after these things that his master's [Potiphar's] wife cast longing eyes on Joseph, and she said, 'Lie with me.'"

Marriage is sacred, and there are boundaries within marriage set by God. Yet how much of the human family is longing for what is outside the boundaries. None of us is immune to temptation, but we don't have to break down those fences. God has always put certain limitations on mankind, even including details such as times and places. Look at Acts 17:26:

"And He has made from one blood every nation of men to dwell on all the face of the earth, and has determined their preappointed times and the boundaries of their dwellings."

God's limitations are ALWAYS for our good.

It seems that human nature is never quite satisfied. We want what we can't have more than we want the abundance we may already have. Further fields look greener. In 1 Timothy 6:6, the Bible talks about *"godliness, with contentment."* There is a Christian perspective to all this. The Apostle Paul expressed it well when he wrote in Philippians 4:11:

"Not that I speak in regard to need, for I have learned in whatever state I am, to be content."

You need to learn contentment. And when you learn to be content, and live a godly life, you may be amazed at the abundance God pours into your life. King David, who also went over the fence to get involved with Bathsheba, learned his lesson well. So well, in fact, that he later wrote in Psalm 107:9:

"For He satisfies the longing soul, and fills the hungry soul with goodness."

If you are longing for the greener fields on the other side of the fence, hear a word of advice. The only thing that makes distant fields look greener, is the perspective. Even a thinly-grassed field looks good from a low angle.

So get your perspective right. Get it higher, and be content with what God has put inside your own boundaries.

So, let's aim to be content, but not insensitive to the needs of others. Perhaps, as Christians, we are content. In that case, we should pay more attention to our godliness as a nation. For *"godliness with contentment is great gain."* Even for a nation!

YOU MAY LOOK DIFFERENT, BUT YOU'RE VALUABLE

Not every egg looks like an egg. I've got a most curious egg that looks like a banana — a white banana, that is. You can peel a banana and you can peel an egg. But this is one "banana-that-looks-like-an-egg" that you should boil before you peel! (I'm not recommending you boil bananas, but I do recommend you read on.)

When I visited the Kornelsen Chicken Farm in British Columbia, I saw a spectacular egg like I had never ever seen in my life before. Of course, it was just one of about 14,000 eggs that day; some of which came in slightly larger or smaller sizes than average. Nevertheless, they were all shaped like eggs. But this particular egg was an outcast. It would not fit normally into an egg carton, and it immediately caused suspicion in the eye of the beholder. It was a mystery. It was different. And, let's face it, anything that is not understood usually causes a tremor of mistrust, fear and, sometimes, even a violent reaction.

Maybe you're not like that. But my first reaction is caution to anything that's out of the ordinary. And if I can't get a handle on it nor understand what's going on, I back off a bit. Fear of the unknown, or fear of the different, can run pretty deep — affecting the way you act and react.

Well, back to the egg I was talking about. It looks like a banana as far as shape is concerned. But, it is an egg. Now if you got an egg that looked like this particular one, would you crack this into the frying pan along with the other normal eggs? Wouldn't you get a little dish, aside from the frying pan, and break it into that first to be on the safe side? What would you do with this very different egg, even when you know with absolute certainty that it actually is a chicken egg?

Do you know what I'd do? I would do what most of the human family would probably do. I would not quite trust it. And why? Because it's a little different.

This is how we sometimes treat people. An egg is an egg. It's shape, size and colour doesn't change that fact. If it came from a bird, it is an egg. (Well, other things come from a chicken too, but you know what I mean). And just because a person is different in colour, shape, size or appearance, doesn't change a thing. Look at what Jesus said in John 7:24:

"Do not judge according to appearance, but judge with righteous judgment."

The Apostle Paul repeated much the same thing about discriminating against other Christians. Just because they don't act or appear quite the same as you would expect doesn't change a thing. Read 2 Corinthians 10:7 with me:

"Do you look at things according to the outward appearance? If anyone is convinced in himself that he is Christ's, let him again consider this in himself, that just as he is Christ's, even so we are Christ's."

We have no right to exclude people just because of their outward appearance, whether it's their colour, clothes, or the way they worship God. We can't see their hearts, nor can we read a person's heart merely by what we see on the outside. Only God knows their hearts, and it's His place to judge the heart. Look at 1 Samuel 16:7:

"For the Lord does not see as man sees; for man looks at the outward appearance, but the Lord looks at the heart."

How quick we are to reject someone just because they don't fit our mould. That egg was an egg, and just because it doesn't look like most eggs doesn't change that fact. It was an egg! Whether you like it or not, an egg is an egg. The Pharisees in Jesus' time rejected Him simply because He didn't fit their preconceived notions — the mould into which the Messiah must fit. Look at John 9:16:

"Therefore some of the Pharisees said, 'This Man is not from God, because He does not keep the Sabbath.' Others said, 'How can a man who is a sinner do such signs?' And there was a division among them."

Just because people don't fit your notion of good and acceptable, doesn't make them of any less value. They are valuable to God. That was a real egg, no matter how odd it may have seemed!

THE STARTING PLACE

The garden looked really nice last summer. It was weeded, carefully watered, and protected against disease and the encroachment of new weeds. But inevitably, some weeds got started so close to the roots of the plants I wanted to protect, that it would have been dangerous to uproot them for fear of destroying the life of the very plant I wanted to protect. So what did I do?

Starting a life needs a lot of care. The only life that never had a beginning and has no end, is the life of God Himself. He is the Great Source of life, even for a garden such as mine.

Everything on earth must have its beginning. Take my beautiful neat rows of plants. Every one of them is an individual little life which started with one little individual seed. All of them are nicely organized into rows, almost like church pews; comparatively straight and almost, but not quite, weed-free.

Very few of them started out in the garden. Most of them started in the little greenhouse (which happens to be white in this case). Every seed was carefully placed into either a peat pot or a little plastic container with soil. Every one of them received individual care. Fertilizer was added with the water and, while cold weather swirled around outside, they were protected inside this greenhouse with heat by night and the sun by day. When little weeds appeared in any of the little peat pots, they were immediately pulled out to leave all the resources of the soil to feed the little seedlings.

A greenhouse is a protected environment. With proper care and fertilization, strong healthy plants can be set out into the more challenging atmosphere of the wind, rain, storms and the challenge of more varieties of weeds which will try to choke them out of existence.

Yet someone had to plant the seeds originally and had to water, weed and protect them from the dangers. But when all was said and done, none of it would have happened unless the seeds had germinated. And that's one thing I have no control over whatsoever.

I cannot help but see a real parallel between this and the life of the Church of Jesus Christ.

When seed is planted, it is as good as dead and buried. Unless God gives it life, it remains in the ground only to rot and be useless. But listen to how God incubates a new life through the Word of God, which the Bible calls "seed." Read John 12:24 with me:

"Most assuredly, I say to you, unless a grain of wheat falls into the ground and dies, it remains alone; but if it dies, it produces much grain."

A greenhouse is in essence a place of death. Every seed sown in here dies. But with proper care, the new life springs up. So it is when a person becomes a Christian. A person must die to themselves — to their own will and ambitions. Then God steps in and gives life, growth and fruitfulness.

When that new life is set out into the challenge of living for God in a world of weeds and wild weather, it still needs care. That's why churches, pastors and fellow Christians are so essential to continued growth and fruitfulness. But real care must be taken on these new lives that have been rooted and grounded in Christ. Some weeds grow so close to the roots of these young plants that to uproot the weeds, you also endanger the life of the plant you want to bear fruit. Look at Matthew 13:27-30:

"So the servants of the owner came and said to him, 'Sir, did you not sow good seed in your field? How then does it have tares?' He said to them, 'An enemy has done this.' The servants said to him, 'Do you want us then to go and gather them up?' But he said, 'No, lest while you gather up the tares you also uproot the wheat with them. Let both grow together until the harvest, and at the time of harvest I will say to the reapers, First gather together the tares and bind them in bundles to burn them, but gather the wheat into my barn.'"

When we see faults or weeds in a new Christian's life, let's be very careful that we don't endanger that new life by violently trying to uproot the unhealthy growth around them. Better to maintain life, than to kill it by overzealous criticism!

PRUNING SEASON

Have you ever wondered if trees can feel pain? I'm not sure they do, but it is an interesting philosophical question. I wouldn't be surprised if some government somewhere has granted a few million dollars to someone who wanted to find out (to what purpose, I don't know). But if trees do feel pain, I'm afraid I'm going to cause some pain by pruning fruit trees. Why? So they'll bear better and more fruit.

There's always something to demand your attention, even on a small acreage like mine. If it's not the goats or the chickens, it's the gardens, the compost, the grass to cut, or any number of repairs to pens, fences and the barn. Most of it is summer work, but winter also has its demands!

February is the time to prune my fruit trees. I'm not really the most expert person to prune trees, but I do know a few things about the job. I've read a few books, and last year I must have done all right because of the results.

Pruning causes a better crop in the following summer. The life and strength of the tree goes into large and healthy fruit, rather than into branches with lots of leaves and small apples, plums, pears or peaches. The energy of the tree can be wasted on fruitless growth.

One of the most useless of all growths on a tree are commonly called "suckers." And that's quite literally what they are: "suckers"! They suck the life and energy out of the main branches, reducing their effective growth of fruit. They are useless and rarely, if ever, grow any fruit at all. They usually grow up from the roots or from main branches straight up as a single long shoot, covered with leaves. They shade the fruit-bearing branches and cut down the free flow of air and sunshine through the tree. Lots of flowing fresh air and sunshine are vital to a tree.

The best and only thing to do is cut them off and throw them away. So the pruning shears have to cut it away. Sometimes this includes the removal of whole branches, not just those annoying yearly suckers.

With that in mind, it really seems to me that when Jesus talked to His followers about pruning and bearing fruit, it must have been a pretty serious business to the Lord. Listen to what He says in John 15:1-2:

"I am the true vine, and My Father is the vinedresser. Every branch in Me that does not bear fruit He takes away; and every branch that bears fruit He prunes, that it may bear more fruit."

Some branches are a part of the tree or vine, yet they are useless unless they bear fruit. The suckers, even though they are on healthy, fruit-bearing branches (no matter how healthy and pretty they may appear) have got to go.

Now there are two ways of looking at the fruit. One way is to see the fruit in the form of edible, useful products such as apples, apricots or plums. That is what is wanted and desired. There is another way of looking at fruit, especially as Christians, and that is the "fruit" of the Spirit. These are the things that make up one's character, personal quality, and true depth of spirituality. There's a whole list of them found in Galatians 5:22-23:

"But the fruit of the Spirit is love, joy, peace, longsuffering, kindness, goodness, faithfulness, gentleness, self-control. Against such there is no law."

As Christians, you and I must examine ourselves from time to time to determine whether or not we are actually bearing fruit of *both kinds!* If we're just suckers and hangers-on, we have no claim on the life of the main trunk or vine. But if we *do* bear fruit, we have every right in the world to draw life from the vine. Look at what Jesus went on to say in John 15:4,6:

"Abide in Me, and I in you. As the branch cannot bear fruit of itself, unless it abides in the vine, neither can you, unless you abide in Me.... If anyone does not abide in Me, he is cast out as a branch and is withered; and they gather them and throw them into the fire, and they are burned."

The implications are pretty far-reaching. So let's take time to see whether we're all show (leaves) or whether we are really walking and living a fruitful life in Jesus Christ.

GOOD CAN COME OUT OF BAD

Some things are right forever, at any place, any time. When I was a youngster, I used to wonder how the Inuits could possibly live in little houses made of blocks of snow. But when I read a *National Geographic* magazine years ago, it was pointed out that snow is a great insulator. The inside of an igloo could be adequately heated by quite a small flame. I never dreamed in all my life that this little piece of knowledge would one day turn out to my good.

I had a strange experience one day out in the barn. I had a fire going in the wood stove, and the temperature was quite acceptable to work away on my lathe at one end of the barn. It was about 15 degrees Celsius. I split some more wood for the fire, stacked it, then decided to check on the chickens and goats. I went to the other end of the barn where the big doors are. They are large enough to let a small truck or car into the barn. But they are also loose fitting and terribly draughty.

Well, that day was a blustery, windy and wild day. Snow was blowing in under the big sliding doors, and had actually piled up a few inches deep. Yet the temperature at the other end of the barn was very comfortable: cold at one end of the barn; warm at the other. Then I remembered that snow is a great insulator. So, what appeared to be a real problem, turned out to be a blessing. I simply shoved the snow up against the big space under the door and packed it in. Suddenly, no draft, and the barn warmed up quite a bit more. If the Inuits can do it, so can I! If they could survive in the old days in an igloo, I could survive in my barn.

I am saving wood and keeping the heat inside the barn. What appeared like a threat, became the solution to a problem!

Life has many opportunities like this. But our attitude toward these situations decides whether this is an insurmountable problem, or an opportunity for imagination and invention. And let's face it, attitude is really a matter of the heart. Listen to what Jesus said in Matthew 12:35:

"A good man out of the good treasure of his heart brings forth good things, and an evil man out of the evil treasure brings forth evil things."

If the heart is good, challenges become opportunities. If the heart is bad, a challenge becomes a curse.

There's an interesting account about Joseph. His jealous brothers wanted to kill him but decided to throw him into a pit. Then he was sold as a slave into Egypt. And his troubles were not over. He was thrown into prison on false charges. Everything in life seemed filled with failure, problems and despair. Yet, through it all, Joseph maintained a positive attitude. His attitude was not just an asset in prison, but also gave him favour when he eventually worked for the King of Egypt. Then later on, when Joseph finally met his hateful brothers, this is what he said to them in Genesis 50:20:

"But as for you, you meant evil against me; but God meant it for good, in order to bring it about as it is this day, to save many people alive."

I thought I was pretty smart when I solved the draughty problem in my barn with the very thing that seemed to be a curse: snow! As a matter of fact, I still think it was a great idea. But that's just me. You should see what happens when God gets involved in a bad situation....

Once, in the history of Israel, Balaam, a maverick prophet, tried to bring ruin and a curse on Israel. But listen to what happened when God took control. It's in Deuteronomy 23:5:

"Nevertheless the Lord your God would not listen to Balaam, but the Lord your God turned the curse into a blessing for you, because the Lord your God loves you."

You don't have to accept the status quo. Your circumstances don't need to have control of you. With the help of God, you can take control of the circumstances, and what appears like a real mess, can eventually bless! The Lord your God loves you!

The next time you face a problem, don't collapse in defeat! Call on God who loves you, and ask Him for help and wisdom. Let's face it, all we can see is the evidence, the circumstance, the problem. But God, who sees and knows the beginning from the end, can see past the problem and the curse to the blessing that He will bring out of it.

Give Him a chance by maintaining a positive attitude.

Chapter 7

Church? What's The Point?

THE ONE DEAD CHICK

Independence is not a very viable option for a chick that is just a few days old. All kinds of harm can come, including cold weather, a hawk, a fox, or even eating the wrong diet. It's not really a good option for grown up chickens either, since with a large flock more eyes are available to detect the dangers. Independence can kill you. And let's face it, no one wants to get "dead!"

I remember a sad day in the "chick" house. I think it was a case of a chick that was too independent to keep together with the little growing flock. Accidents happen more often when there's no one to warn and help!

Let me start at the beginning. As I mentioned, we brought 50 new lives into the care of the Bombay clan: chicks. They started out in a small box, heated with two light bulbs. When they were very small, the box walls were too high for them to get out. Then as growth took place, some of them did get out of the box and, besides, it was getting a little crowded. So I took the box out, leaving the two light bulbs as a beacon so they could always get home. They were allowed a larger space to move about. I also put in a small space heater to heat the larger area. The food was in one place, and the water in another. Yet, all of these provisions were accessible to all. The chicks were free to move from one place to another, and then back into their community under the warm lights.

Well, the next day when I got home, the space heater had run out of fuel. All the chicks were a bit cold, but were well-fed and warmly cuddled together. That is all except one. It lay stiff as a stick and dead, off by itself. It did not go back to the warmth of the two lights, nor to the comfortable closeness of the 49 other chicks. On its own, independently, it died from the cold.

We lose chicks when they think they can get along without the rest of the flock. Inside the barn, it could be due to the cold. Outside the barn, it could be the result of a predator. Independence is dangerous and it can kill.

It's really not much different from a local congregation of Christians. Occasionally, there are members who feel they don't need the rest of the flock. They are just a mite independent, and they feel they can get all the food they need by reading the Bible by themselves. What about the need for water? Well, they say they can also pray by themselves. Either way, they make it clear that they can get along without the rest of the Church.

They say, "I can get along without the pastor! I report directly to God, don't you know? I can stand alone and, besides, the pastor's just human like me!"

The Bible has some advice for such folk, and with some very good reasons. Look at Hebrews 10:24-25:

"And let us consider one another in order to stir up love and good works, not forsaking the assembling of ourselves together, as is the manner of some, but exhorting one another, and so much the more as you see the Day approaching."

Christian fellowship is essential for survival, because there are some cold days from time to time. Think of the attempts to wipe out the Church of Jesus Christ in times past. They had strength when they stayed together in fellowship and support.

Anyone who says they don't need the pastor or other Christians is living absolutely contrary to the teachings of the Word of God. Look at Ephesians 4:11:

"And He Himself gave some to be apostles, some prophets, some evangelists, and some pastors and teachers, for the equipping of the saints for the work of ministry, for the edifying of the Body of Christ, till we all come to the unity of the faith and the knowledge of the Son of God, to a perfect man, to the measure of the stature of the fullness of Christ...."

The Apostle Paul goes to great lengths to point out that the Body of Christ, the Church, is totally interdependent. We must have each other. When we become separated from other believers and try to stand alone, the cold days will come when there's no one to lean on for strength and warmth of fellowship. Then what? You're dead!

Paul ends his argument with a simple statement in 1 Corinthians 12:18:

"But now God has set the members, each one of them, in the Body just as He pleased."

Stand alone, and you're one dead chick!

SO, WHAT'S FOR DINNER?

One thing about our house is that no one is starving to death. And that's not because all three of us who live in the house are graduates from colleges where the Bible formed the largest part of the curriculum. We're all fair cooks. Mary, of course, excels and I "swells." But what about the house where no food is prepared, even though it's sitting there in the fridge already? Or, just as bad, what about the Church where the pulpit is unprepared?

"So, what's for dinner?" I asked Mary the other day. "I don't know, I haven't given it a thought!" she answered.

Well, she can't be blamed for that, since she has more than enough to do these days. Besides taking care of things around our house, she is busy looking after young grandson Joshua sometimes while our son's household is getting used to another cause of busyness: little, beautiful, quiet, Victoria Alexandra. She may be quiet, but she still needs her bottle, diaper changes, loving and holding and all that goes with a new baby.

So Mary fills in the gaps at this point and doesn't get home until just shortly before dinner herself. So when I asked, "What's for dinner?" it was more my stomach talking than my head. But as you all know, the way to a man's stomach is right through the front of his head!

Three people live in our house. We're all busy, what with jobs and other ministry involvements from which we too often come home tired. But with three people, we have three potential cooks. Potential, I say, because we're not sure who might put the meal together when we get home. If Mary's home on time, she prepares a real nice meal — the nicest being spaghetti and meatballs, of course! This is always delicious, especially when served with beet pickles as a side dish.

But any good meal as anyone knows, takes a bit of preparation. You just don't take the first four things you find in the fridge and throw them into a pot of water and boil away. A half-filled jar of strawberry jam would just float, in any case! Of course not! You pick and choose and plan a balanced meal. Then you heat it up.

First decision with discernment, then action with attention. Then, finally, presentation!

This is like preparing a good sermon. I've known pastors who go into the pulpit unprepared and, as a result, congregations go home undernourished. How do I know this, you may ask? Because people write me letters. I've also listened occasionally as an unprepared meal was served.

My advice? Pray for your pastor. When's the last time you prepared your pastor for a sermon? You should encourage and pray for him or her. And, on the other hand, if your pastor is not feeding you, you have two choices: eat from your own garden by reading the Bible daily and letting God's Word nourish you, or find a table that has been prepared (where a pastor goes into the pulpit prepared or where there is a Bible study group that nourishes the soul). You can't live on pizza forever.

Some people want me to write to their pastors. Sorry, that's your responsibility. They are responsible to God, their own spiritual leaders, and to you. If you ask them what's for dinner, and they answer that they've not given it a thought, you have a problem. It's really a matter of love: love for God and love for God's people. If that's missing, you've got a problem. People perish without a knowledge of God.

First let's look at part of a conversation between Pastor Peter and Jesus. It's found in John 21:17:

"He said to him the third time, 'Simon, son of Jonah, do you love Me?' Peter was grieved because He said to him the third time, 'Do you love Me?' And he said to Him, 'Lord, You know all things; You know that I love You.' Jesus said to him, 'Feed My sheep.'"

Even for sheep, some preparation has to be made. You don't just turn them loose in the field, you guide them to good pasture. And good pasture for the Christian is growing in the knowledge and grace of our Lord Jesus Christ. In Hosea 4:6, we read:

"My people are destroyed for lack of knowledge. Because you have rejected knowledge, I also will reject you from being priests for Me; Because you have forgotten the law of your God, I also will forget your children."

God has appointed in the Church, pastors and teachers. If they are not pastoring and teaching, perhaps they're not appointed by God.

Hungry? Go where there's food!

IF YOU DON'T, SOMEONE ELSE WILL!

When I saw a little scarlet-necked hummingbird darting about outside my front window, it almost ruined my night's sleep. It had returned from the south and was looking at an empty place where last year it came to feed. I was totally exhausted, but it bothered me. So as weary as I was, I got out the long ladder, prepared and hung the little hummingbird feeder. I did my duty. I slept well that night. How are *you* sleeping these nights?

After getting home from the office one day, I spent three hours cutting the lawn, and had begun to dig a small area for a little fish pond in our back yard. I thought it would be a nice place where Mary and I could just sit and have a lemonade on a hot summer's day. When I finally went into the house at about 8:30 p.m., dusk was just settling. I was exhausted. I had been at the office that morning since 6:10 a.m. I had put in a long, hard day. Now I just wanted to relax.

Then something interrupted my quiet. As I looked out across the lawn, suddenly I saw a hummingbird dart up to the window, circle a few times in the place where we had a hummingbird feeder last year. It had obviously come back north and wanted a little sweetness. But there was nothing there!

I didn't want to move. But I could only stand it for about three minutes. I got up, wearily carried the ladder to the house from the barn, cleaned and filled the hummingbird feeder, and hung it in its accustomed place.

Well, the next evening when I got home from the office and had done all the chores, I sat down again in my accustomed place. Sure enough, the hummingbirds were back; their little scarlet necks reflecting the sun and their little wings beating away in a blur. My little flock was back and they were safe. They have settled in for a long summer with us.

Yet, I could have neglected them. I could have given in to my weariness and just left them to fend for themselves. In all likelihood, they would have survived somehow. But I am a pastor at heart. Not to just a little flock of hummingbirds, but to people. And if I don't provide food, someone else might — and it could be a very bad diet!

Pastors have an awesome responsibility. And it's not easy. After a long hard day, it's not always easy to respond to the needs of people. Exhaustion can, and does, come to pastors. They need a holiday, and they need someone who will conscientiously feed the flock while they're away. I had the honour of filling in for a pastor recently while he was away for a well-deserved rest. And he's the kind of pastor I'd prefer for (even while on holidays) he telephoned back several times just to be sure all was well.

Unfortunately, not all pastors are as faithful. In fact, God sent a prophet to castigate some pastors (or, as Paul called them, "Shepherds of the flock"). It's found in the Old Testament in Jeremiah 23:2:

"Therefore thus says the Lord God of Israel against the shepherds who feed My people: 'You have scattered My flock, driven them away, and not attended to them. Behold, I will attend to you for the evil of your doings,' says the Lord."

Not a nice prospect, but it does illustrate the awesome responsibility a pastor has to his flock, and to the Great Shepherd Himself. Look at what the prophet Micah said about the coming Messiah:

"And He shall stand and feed His flock in the strength of the Lord, in the majesty of the name of the Lord His God; and they shall abide, for now He shall be great to the ends of the earth" (Micah 5:4).

And Jesus, the "Great Shepherd" of the sheep has passed that immediate responsibility on to your pastor, and it is quite clearly illustrated by that embarrassingly personal encounter between Jesus and Peter. Let's look again at John 21:17:

"He said to him the third time, 'Simon, son of Jonah, do you love Me?' Peter was grieved because He said to him the third time, 'Do you love Me?' And he said to Him, 'Lord, You know all things; You know that I love You.' Jesus said to him, 'Feed My sheep.'"

And let's face it, the soul of one child of God is of more value than a hummingbird!

RECOGNIZE THE SHEPHERD (or Goatherd)

I can tell the difference between goats and sheep. One thing is the tail — and do I have a tale to tell! But how does a sheep or a goat recognize its shepherd (or goatherd, as the case may be). Of course, once you have been in the Shepherd's care for a while, you come to recognize and trust Him. That's the Great Shepherd. But what about the new shepherd (or pastor, as the case may be)? How do you know he's really okay? Good question, right? Answer coming up!

Whenever I go out to the goats, they approach me really cautiously. They seem to remember one day when I was fixing a fence. One of them came up behind me and started chewing on the back of my trousers. At first, I simply pulled away from her, and she backed off. As I continued working on the fence she came up behind me and, once again, began her bad eating habit. I swung a hand around behind me and connected with her horn and the side of her head. I probably hurt myself more than her, but at least I still had pants on when I went back into the house.

This particular goat must still remember this incident as she's still cautious with me. When my daughter Elaine approaches the two of them they both trot right up to her and follow her around as though she's a kindly shepherd. As I thought about it, they probably *do* consider her to be their protector, feeder and provider, since they are her goats and she looks after them more than I do. They seem to recognize and trust their own shepherd more than me.

A lady wrote to me the other day and told me of her experience with her chickens. I don't know where people get the idea I have any interest in chickens. Well, of course, I just bought another 50 baby chicks! In any case, she told me that she always wore exactly the same skirt and jacket when she went out to attend her chickens. They were never disturbed at all. She moved among them freely, collected the eggs, fed them and watered them — all without any commotion.

One day she was giving herself some kind of facial treatment. She had applied some white paste or something to her face and had to wait for 20 minutes before she took it off. (I'm sure you ladies will understand about this. I sure don't.) Anyway, she put her usual skirt and jacket on, and went out to the chickens. They went crazy, scattering all over the place. A stranger was among them. This was not safe! That white stuff on her face, instead of the usual face with the usual skirt and jacket, got them wired and wary. They didn't recognize their shepherd.

There is a good lesson here: learn to recognize your shepherd. In fact, there are two shepherds we really need to recognize and feel comfortable with. One is the Great Shepherd of the sheep, Jesus. And the other is an "under-shepherd": your pastor. You should feel comfortable with both because both are appointed by God for your welfare. First of all, let's look at Jesus' words in John 10:11:

"I am the Good Shepherd. The Good Shepherd gives His life for the sheep."

In Hebrews 13:20-21, we see Him once again as a friend beyond the call of duty. He deserves our trusting response. Let's read it:

"Now may the God of peace who brought up our Lord Jesus from the dead, that Great Shepherd of the sheep, through the blood of the everlasting covenant, make you complete in every good work to do His will, working in you what is well pleasing in His sight, through Jesus Christ, to whom be glory forever and ever. Amen."

Now that's pretty straight forward. But how do I know I can really trust the pastor, especially if I'm new in the church? Well, here's how! They, too, have been given instructions so that you can recognize the genuine article. Look at Acts 20:28:

"Therefore take heed to yourselves and to all the flock, among which the Holy Spirit has made you overseers, to shepherd the Church of God which He purchased with His own blood."

Pastors must recognize their flocks as the precious purchased possessions of God.

Another instruction pastors have received and must obey, is found in 1 Peter 5:2:

"Shepherd the flock of God which is among you, serving as overseers, not by constraint but willingly, not for dishonest gain but eagerly."

If your pastor is reluctant to give you time, and has more than six Cadillacs, be careful. Shepherds need to be faithful and trustworthy — and not slap you around!

GROWING SEASON

When I went out to my gardens one Sunday, I couldn't help but see the great similarity between a garden and a church congregation. There is great variety, each is susceptible to different pests, and all are in need of rain and sun. Fighting off all the enemies of a garden is a tough job. Pastoring a congregation with its great variety of people is really very similar. If you think pastors don't sweat, keep reading. I've got news for you....

What a summer! It started with plenty of rain. The sunshine was neither too much nor too little. When it was dry for a few weeks, I was able to irrigate enough to keep things growing. As a result, I have vegetables coming out my ears. No, let me change that: ears are coming out of my garden (ears of corn, that is)! My garden is overflowing with peas, carrots, cabbage, rhubarb, strawberries, raspberries, apples, three varieties of corn, pumpkin, broccoli, lettuce, Swiss chard, beets, squash, cucumbers, cantaloupe, watermelon, green peppers, okra, potatoes, yellow wax beans and, yes, bushels of big tomatoes.

But in spite of the almost perfect weather, it didn't all come easily. I had to plant it all in the first place. Then there was the weeding, watering and thinning. And, of course, there were pests: raccoons, opossum, slugs, caterpillars, corn borers, blue jays, robins and other small varmints. All these had to be controlled or banned in one way or another. I can witness to the fact that God spoke truly when He told Adam in Genesis 3:19:

"In the sweat of your face you shall eat bread...."

There is a great similarity in all this to the pastoring of a church. Unlike a garden, the church is not filled with vegetables! However, there is a tremendous variety of people and personalities in any church. Each individual has personal needs, pains and problems. The wise pastor doesn't just stand in the pulpit and water them with the Word on Sundays. He also gets involved in the personal needs of their lives. In other words, he helps get rid of the weeds. Sometimes a church member gets too involved in too many things, and this impedes his spiritual growth. That's when a pastor is called upon to give some wisdom in weeding out the nonessentials so real growth can take place and, of course, the preaching of the Word. Paul told Pastor Timothy, in 2 Timothy 4:2:

"Preach the Word! Be ready in season and out of season. Convince, rebuke, exhort, with all longsuffering and teaching."

If you think the responsibilities of a pastor are light and easy, let me assure you, a great sweat will often break out on the face of a pastor who is really courageous enough to fulfil his calling. Exhorting is not too awfully difficult, but rebuking is a little more challenging and often necessary.

I am disturbed by the number of letters I have received from people who either feel their pastor is no good, or from others who feel their pastor is under attack, criticism and pressure. Pastors do not have an easy task. THEY are the ones who call people to repentance. THEY are the ones who have to confront sin. THEY are the ones who have to step in with love to a hateful situation. And even more importantly, they have been put in place by God. Listen to Ephesians 4:11-13:

"And He Himself gave some to be apostles, some prophets, some evangelists, and some pastors and teachers, for the equipping of the saints for the work of ministry, for the edifying of the Body of Christ, till we all come to the unity of the faith and the knowledge of the Son of God, to a perfect man, to the measure of the stature of the fullness of Christ."

No, I'm not saying every pastor is perfect. But I am saying they have a tough and, often, thankless job. We, as people in the pew, can make it either easier or harder for them. And just in case you tend to be a thistle in the garden, let me point out what God said through the psalmist David in Psalm 105:15:

"...do not touch My anointed ones, and do My prophets no harm."

So, the next time you go out to your garden to look at the variety there and realize the work you've put into it, think of your pastor with gratitude to God, and pray for him or her.

Chapter 8

Fine-Feathered Friends

BE CAREFUL, THERE'S DANGER!

There is drama at the feeder. Birds, fully aware of a waiting cat that is poised to strike, still take the risk of their lives just for a piece of cracked corn or wheat. Good food is available in a thousand other places, but they come to where it's easier to get and also where the danger is most threatening. And the feathers left at our back door prove that there are always some who lose in this gamble with life.

I saw a drama unfold in our front yard, just about 20 feet from our living room window. I was up early that Sunday morning. It's a habit I've been in for years. During the week, I usually get to the office earlier than most. And the habit of rising early continues, even on Saturday and Sunday mornings. This particular morning, as I was reading my Bible and occasionally glancing out at the rising sun and the lightening day, I heard a blue jay giving a warning cry. It was sitting on top of the bird feeder, nervously hopping around and crying out warnings. Other jays would occasionally swoop down close to the feeder, sometimes even landing there for a moment, then off to a tree or our housetop.

Finally, I found the reason. Elaine's cat, under a nearby spruce tree, lay dead still. Not a hair moved. Its tail was tucked and motionless. Unblinking eyes. Not the flicker of an ear. Perfectly motionless. The jay finally hopped lower to the feeding rail. Still the cat remained motionless. The jay hopped around to the far side of the feeder, furthest away from the cat. As soon as it did, like a flash, the cat was in the air, feet spread, ready to swat whatever part of the jay was exposed. A very near miss.

The jay was gone. The cat remained for a moment where it landed, then slowly crept back under the spruce. Again it sat there, absolutely motionless. And the jay, disregarding all past experience, returned to the feeder. Its hunger for some seed overcame its caution.

We have found the feathers of blue jays and other birds at the back door: trophies of the success of a patient cat lying in wait for one incautious act of a bird. You'd think that the love of life itself would take precedence over the need for a bit of cracked corn. It's not as though there are no other sources of food. Our cats bring trophies from more places than the feeder. (In fact, I'm not sure they've ever caught a bird at the feeder. It's too high!) Though the birds are not ignorant of the cat's intentions, they just keep flirting with danger.

So it is like people! Christians, I mean. They flirt with the traps set for them by the enemy. They act as though Satan has given up on them and they are beyond his reach. Yet the apostle has this warning for us all, found in 1 Peter 5:8:

"Be sober, be vigilant; because your adversary the devil walks about like a roaring lion, seeking whom he may devour."

Unfortunately, he's successfully done it sometimes. We all know of those whose lives have been crushed and ruined by the tricks of the enemy. They flirted too intimately with the very things we all know are dangerous to our eternal welfare. Somehow, we assume we are immune. But Paul warns us in 2 Corinthians 2:11 to be careful:

"...lest Satan should take advantage of us; for we are not ignorant of his devices."

Evil is a reality. There are real dangers. The threat of death and destruction are all around us. And in that area of our lives where our spiritual welfare is at risk, we often act very naively. We somehow assume spiritual threat is less serious than physical threat.

I have never met a person in my life, unless they were totally suicidal, who would deliberately try to walk across a sixteen-lane highway, without at least trying to dodge speeding cars. It's stupid. Yet we seem to forget that the Bible warns us very clearly about Satan in John 10:10:

"The thief does not come except to steal, and to kill, and to destroy. I have come that they may have life, and that they may have it more abundantly."

And Satan doesn't go away. He waits quietly; unmoving until he has his chance. Then he pounces. And just like our cat, he parades the feathers that remain and leaves them at our back door as a trophy of his destructive and devouring nature. Yet we go on risking the abundant life that is ours through Jesus Christ.

You'd think we'd learn. Especially when the feathers are still blowing around us from the last victim!

Two hours later, I looked out the window. The cat was still waiting, ready to pounce. Be careful!

IT TAKES A WHILE BEFORE YOU GET IT RIGHT!

It's an interesting thing to watch the seeming confusion in the actions of a new young hen that has just laid her first egg. If it survives the drop, she walks around it, eyes it from every angle, clucks and chuckles about it for a while, then seems to walk away bewildered. When a new layer is bewildered, she needs help from an experienced example. Although some may question this statement, I've never laid an egg. So I call in the experts: old experienced hens. They'll help them to get it right!

At about five months, chickens go through a strange and traumatic change. All their first growth of feathers start to fall out. It's called moulting (but I forgot to warn them that this would happen). New and better feathers begin to replace them. Life takes on a new dimension and much to their surprise, something inside also begins to change. They want to eat more, but they don't seem to gain much weight. In fact, they get this strange mothering instinct which, at first, they don't even know how to handle.

One day, every one of them to their further surprise, instinctively wants to sit and nest for a little while. A strange sensation overwhelms them and, in a kind of stupor, they feel something happening back at their stern end. They rise slightly and to their shock and surprise, something gently falls out of them. It's called an egg.

Now depending on where they chose to nest, the egg can end up in one of several conditions. One of these new young ladies had her stern hanging over the edge of a two-by-four, six feet off the ground when she first had this amazing experience. Looking down, she saw a mess. Other hens came to inspect it, then decided it looked good enough to eat, so this is what they did.

Another hen was sitting out in the chicken run for her first egg. She turned around, inspected it from various angles, and finally left it in the sun. It was a big egg. When I broke it open, it had two little yolks in it. She hadn't got this thing right yet.

The next day, one of the hens who happened to be sitting on a feed bin had the same experience. She eyed it for a while, and then left it to look after itself. Even for chickens, it takes a little while to get it right. I have nests in various places throughout the coop, built just for their comfort and the protection of these new products.

It finally seems to dawn on them that they used to be inside of those brown things called eggs, and that these new things should be protected. In another week or two, they'll get it all figured out, and the laying of eggs will finally be done in a routine and organized manner. After all, you don't expect a six-month-old to have all the answers, do you? So, they needed help. I just opened the door between the old experienced hens, who now mix freely with the new hens. The younger set now have an example to follow.

It's the same with people. Newborns coming into the kingdom of God make mistakes. They mess up once in a while. They need help. And that's where older, experienced Christians can come in real handy. They can help them grow up and learn the right way of doing things, by example. But there is a way for us older Christians to go about it. Sometimes there are tensions between the young and the old, just like with my chickens. But we find in Ephesians 4:15-16 how to go about it:

"...speaking the truth in love, [that we] may grow up in all things into Him who is the head — Christ — from whom the whole Body, joined and knit together by what every joint supplies, according to the effective working by which every part does its share, causes growth of the Body for the edifying of itself in love."

The flock becomes one in spirit and in purpose and, yes, even in product. But we, who are older Christians, need to be warned. Listen to 2 Peter 3:17-18:

"You therefore, beloved, since you know this beforehand, beware lest you also fall from your own steadfastness, being led away with the error of the wicked; but grow in the grace and knowledge of our Lord and Saviour Jesus Christ. To Him be the glory both now and forever. Amen."

Let's not peck at new and stumbling Christians. Instead, let's just set an example, love them, and grow with them.

CLIPPING THEIR WINGS

I would never have done it if it hurt them. But it didn't hurt them! It just scared them for a moment. When I was finished they found that life was just as normal as always with full freedom within reasonable bounds. I clipped their wings! And if you have a problem with that, you better read on so I can explain.

I guess it all started when several of my chickens came to believe that the grass was greener on the other side of the fence. One got out, by taking a flying leap over the top of the fence. She then began to eat the fresh green grass on the other side. It wasn't long before too many were flying out and feasting on the wonderful green stuff that grows in abundance — both on the lawn and in my gardens.

After one chicken learns a bad habit, it's not long before the rest of them take up the habit. Obviously some corrective action had to be taken. I had several choices. I suppose I could have added another four feet to the fence, but that would mean total captivity and total restriction — legalism at its worst.

So I did the best and cheapest thing. I clipped their wings. This is a painless little procedure. You simply cut off the long feathers on one wing. It's not long before they find that trying to take a flight out of the chicken run ends in a crash course in aeronautics. When one wing won't fly, you can't get lift off!

I've had to do this before. Once always does the job. They try a few times, and when they can't make it, something inside their pea-sized brains comes to the conclusion that they can't fly higher than about two feet. Then they develop the deep and lasting conviction that flying the coop is not an option. And besides, they get all the fresh grass clippings they need every time we mow the lawn. Everything they need is brought in to where they can enjoy full protection and freedom, within reasonable limits.

Sometimes Christians need their wings clipped, especially some of the younger breed who have a streak of rebellious independence and a dangerous longing for self-determination outside the normal fences of safety set up by their parents, pastor, elders and/or spiritual leaders.

That's when the wing-clipping becomes necessary. And sometimes it's a little painful to be brought into obedience within the freedom God does give us. Even Jesus, our High Priest, found this to be true, for we read in Hebrews 5:8:

"...though He was a Son, yet He learned obedience by the things which He suffered."

Sometimes we need our wings clipped for our own good and to keep us within reach of the family of God, which has been called to holiness. In Jesus Christ, we have great liberty. But look at Galatians 5:13:

"For you, brethren, have been called to liberty; only do not use liberty as an opportunity for the flesh, but through love serve one another."

God has provided us with a family — His family — for mutual benefit and strength. But when we get the notion that our personal good is better served by getting outside the fence entirely, we make a grave error. When we present ourselves to the world, we could become slaves to it. Look at Romans 6:16:

"Do you not know that to whom you present yourselves slaves to obey, you are that one's slaves whom you obey, whether of sin leading to death, or of obedience leading to righteousness?"

You have a choice: liberty in Christ or slavery outside Christ. You can either control your own actions as a child of God, or you can subject yourself to the wing-clipping that the Lord sometimes imposes on us until we learn obedience.

Having had my wings clipped a few times, I know what I'm talking about. And so did that great poet who wrote Psalm 119:45. He decided the ball was in his court, and that he'd make a decision. This is what he says:

"And I will walk at liberty, for I seek Your precepts."

It *is* possible to have every single need met, within the fence of God's provision. And inside the safe place, you have total and full freedom. As the Bible says in John 8:36:

"Therefore if the Son makes you free, you shall be free indeed."

Enjoy your liberty in Christ, but don't become a libertine, or you'll possibly get your wings clipped.

THE DEVIL'S A CHICKEN

Did you ever see a chicken win a fight with a full-grown man? Of course not! Chickens are too chicken to take on the authority of a human. They know by their very nature that they're out-classed and totally unable to subdue anything as big as a man. But, once in a while, some rooster will try. He's just trying to "fake you out." He's a liar, and simply trying to make you believe a lie. Just like the devil. He's a liar too, and will try to "fake you out!" And he'll use fear to intimidate you!

Some time ago, my little grandson Joshua was severely frightened by an advertisement on television. It actually traumatized him to a degree. The commercial went something like this: A car was following a truck full of chickens. Something broke loose on the truck arid a whole bunch of chickens crashed onto the windshield of the car. To make matters worse, all of this was recorded on camera.

Well, when Joshua saw this for the first time, he screamed in terror and ran from the room crying. When the commercial was over, he timidly came back into the room. Every time that commercial came on, Josh would run screaming and terrified out of the room or to an adult.

The next time we went to my barn, I asked him to help me collect the eggs. He got as far as the door. When he saw a few white chickens, he ran crying with fear.

I said to Josh, "You don't have to be scared of the chickens because, actually, they are afraid of you." He didn't believe me at first, so I said, "Watch!" As he stood at the door, I suddenly ran into the chicken coop. The chickens scattered in fear. The next time I suggested, "You try it!" Then I took his hand and reassuringly told him, "Let's do it together." And I ran into the chicken coop with Josh's hand in mine. The chickens scattered again. Then I said, "Josh, you run at them alone, and you'll see that they'll be scared of you. You have no reason to be scared of them." After some hesitation he tried it and, sure enough, the chickens flew and scattered away from him in every direction.

Josh walks right in now, even though they walk all around him. If one gets too close, he makes a sudden move and the chicken takes off, like the "chicken" it is. He now knows that chickens are just... well... chickens. All he has to do is assert his little, immature human authority.

Chickens were born chickens. And nothing will change that.

In spite of the fact that all Christians know that Satan was defeated at Calvary and the resurrection of Jesus Christ, they still have an unhealthy fear of the devil. I would like to state categorically, the devil is a defeated foe. He's a chicken. As long as he can lie to you and make you think he has greater power than he has, you'll run every time he raises his ugly head. The mere mention of the Name of Jesus and the victory of the cross and resurrection, will send him (and any of his demons) scurrying for cover. They KNOW they are defeated. It's time that we as Christians began to KNOW of our authority in Jesus Christ. Listen to these absolute assurances from the Scriptures. First of all, look at what Jesus told His disciples even before the crucifixion and resurrection in Matthew 28:18:

"And Jesus came and spoke to them, saying, 'All authority has been given to Me in heaven and on earth.'"

That establishes the fact that Jesus has all authority. Then in Mark 16:17, we read Jesus' words:

"And these signs will follow those who believe: In My name they will cast out demons; they will speak with new tongues...."

The physician Luke records a further delegation of this authority in Luke 9:1:

"Then He called His twelve disciples together and gave them power and authority over all demons, and to cure diseases."

This was all before Calvary. The Bible teaches us that by faith, we have Jesus living in us with all his authority. In James 4:7 we read:

"Therefore submit to God. Resist the devil and he will flee from you."

So you don't have to bend to the lies and deceptions of the devil or any of his little demons. They're defeated, and they know it. And when you resist them in the authority you have in Christ, they'll scatter like the chickens they really are. It's not a power struggle. It's simply the truth. And it's the TRUTH that sets you free!

Now little Joshua eats chicken for lunch! Got the message?

SENSITIVITY

Someone came up to me the other day and mentioned that she really didn't like chickens at all. And why didn't I talk about cats or dogs, which she liked. Well, today, I'm going to talk about my dogs. You see, dogs — at least our dogs — have sensitive ears and are really tuned in to nature all around them. It seems that it's we human beings who have really "gone to the dogs," so to speak. This time, perhaps we can learn something from them. Keep reading for what might be your first obedience training class!

We have three dogs in our little three-and-a-half acre "farmlet." That's one dog per acre. (Although to be mathematically accurate, we should have another half of a dog for the remaining half acre.) They have exceptional hearing. They always recognize the sound of my car or Mary's car, long before it is near the house. They run out with happy yelps and are often in the driveway waiting before you can even see the driveway. Other cars of the same make and model go by, and they show no reaction at all. They seem to be able to distinguish the slight little differences in the sounds of our cars, and recognize them immediately.

Often at night, when there is not a sound as far as we know, they suddenly sit up alert and give a sharp bark or stand stiffly alert, listening intently. They hear what we cannot hear.

Our neighbours have geese. They often honk and call as they wander the property. They have a large pond, and wild geese often settle down into the pond. Usually the dogs pay little or no attention. But once in a while, the calls of the geese, both domesticated and wild, take on a difference tone — a warning of some danger. Our dogs react, become alert, and give sharp barks of warning. There seems to be a sensitivity within nature, where warnings are heard and understood between various species of life.

In many parts of the world, the human family also knows how to interpret the sounds and their true meaning. Anyone familiar with the northland woods also has a keen ear to understand warnings of danger through the sounds of wildlife. Most of the world has totally lost this affinity with nature, and is distracted by sounds of business and commerce, cars and cash registers.

It would be good for the whole world to occasionally take a walk in the woods, and resensitize itself to the voices of nature. Even to understand why a dog barks might be a worthwhile thought to pursue.

I see an unfortunate parallel. And strangely, I see it in the Church.

As Christians, we don't hear the voice of warning which we should heed. We have become desensitized by the busyness of life and work around us, and we have become hardened in our spiritual hearing apparatus.

God has always been ready to speak to His people and to warn us of unknown dangers ahead. Listen to Ezekiel 3:17:

"Son of man, I have made you a watchman for the house of Israel; therefore hear a word from My mouth, and give them warning from Me."

Jesus told us clearly that we should be sensitive to the voice of the Spirit of God for guidance into truth and of things to come in our lives. Look at John 16:13:

"However, when He, the Spirit of truth, has come, He will guide you into all truth; for He will not speak on His own authority, but whatever He hears He will speak; and He will tell you things to come."

Many people spend so little time in prayer, and seem unaware of the voice of God speaking, leading, warning and guiding. They have become calloused and hard of heart. In Hebrews 3:7-9, we read:

"Therefore, as the Holy Spirit says: 'Today, if you will hear His voice, do not harden your hearts as in the rebellion, in the day of trial in the wilderness, where your fathers tested Me, tried Me, and saw My works forty years.'"

Unlike most of nature, which still can hear and understand the sounds and warnings of the rest of nature, we, as Christians, often lose our sensitivity to the voice of the Lord. It seems that new Christians are very sensitive at first. Often (certainly in less than 40 years) we begin to depend on past experience, rather than keeping our relationship to the Lord fresh enough to still hear His voice deep in our spirits.

God help us to never let our conscience become, as the Bible says, *"seared with a hot iron"* and unable to hear Him! Let's not become distracted by business and commerce, cars and cash registers!

A SAD AFFAIR

Well, the old hen — my favourite old hen — passed into the great beyond. That nice little chicken which appears in my arms in the little booklet, *A Funny Thing Happened On The Way To The Barn,* died on the very day that booklet was published. I guess it was just a little more fame than she could handle. But life goes on. I've got 25 young ones just coming over the horizon. And let's face it, the horizon is more exciting than staring at the ground....

Everyone has come to know my favourite chicken: a Plymouth (barred) Rock. The reason I had this particular chicken was that it was the same breed my father had when I was a child. Dad had about a dozen of these hens. So when I had a chance to get a few, I did. It was for sentimental reasons I suppose. But, in any case, she became my favourite hen, and was the most placid and friendly old girl. She faithfully supplied me with good big brown eggs for years.

Well, old age set in and, as they say, all good things come to an end. She died. Now when I see her smiling beak on the booklet we published, I can only remember. There's an empty bunk in the henhouse. It doesn't seem quite the same going out to the henhouse these days. She was such a pretty thing, perhaps a bit superior to the rest of the flock; but, in her old age, she deserved some special treatment. Over the years, she had seen many others come and go. Now, she's gone.

I suppose it was just a coincidence that she died the very day the little booklet was published. That's her in my arms on the front cover and throughout the booklet. I suppose it was also a coincidence that I had just bought another 25 chicks, which will also lay brown eggs. But she'll never be replaced. She was as much a pet as she was an egg producer.

But life goes on. Some good things come to an end. We have to accept simple facts like that. And there's always — and I mean ALWAYS — something that comes along (though it may never fill the void left by the loss) that will provide a new direction, a new interest, a new excitement.

Throughout life this will happen. I can remember losses of great significance to me when I was a child: a bicycle that was stolen, our dog that was poisoned, and a special tee shirt that I had to reluctantly surrender to the garbage pail. But life goes on, even when some good things come to an end.

Loss is not new to mankind. Thousands of years ago, Job had suffered some terrible losses. Look at what he says in Job 17:11:

"My days are past, my purposes are broken off, even the thoughts of my heart."

And then in Job 29:2, we read:

"Oh, that I were as in months past, as in the days when God watched over me...."

We can long for the old days and grieve over some losses. With a chicken, it's really no big deal. But when the chance for salvation dies, it's serious. There was one cry from the heart of God's people, found in Jeremiah 8:20, which rends the heart. Let's read it:

"The harvest is past, the summer is ended, and we are not saved!"

But we can't go on living in the past. Excitement and new adventure is ahead. There are new horizons to explore, no matter how successful you may have already been. In Philippians 3:13-14, Paul says:

"Brethren, I do not count myself to have apprehended; but one thing I do, forgetting those things which are behind and reaching forward to those things which are ahead, I press toward the goal for the prize of the upward call of God in Christ Jesus."

Losing a chicken is one thing, but losing the future is quite another. Loss — and the grief that follows it — is legitimate and healthy to work through. However, you must work through it to your future. You still have one, you know!

So, my favourite chicken has gone. I'm not going to stare at her empty nest. I'm going to watch the next 25 grow up and become my new excitement. And, YOU, don't cast down your eyes to the ground forever. Look up the road and you will see that new happiness is just coming up over the hill!

WASTEFUL, WASTEFUL, WASTEFUL!

There are a few birds who feed at our feeder in front of our living room window, which really upsets me: sparrows and grackles. Their eating habits seem so wasteful. They pick out the best for themselves, and simply throw the rest away by sweeping it off the feeder with their beaks. What a waste. Of course, in this case, the poor ground-feeding birds have the leftovers. There are also times when I wish the human family was organized enough not to waste, but to share their plenty.

I have been back from Africa for seventeen years now, and there's still one thing with which I really struggle in our society. It was brought back to mind as I was watching a grackle, a type of blackbird which often comes to our bird feeder. It has incandescent purple neck feathers which are just plain gorgeous. But it really bothers me with its eating habits. It's picky, picky, picky. It wants cracked corn which is a part of the feed we put out. The majority of the feed is grain; chiefly wheat with some sunflower seeds. This wasteful bird sweeps out all the grain it doesn't want with its beak until a piece of corn appears, which it gulps down. Wasteful, wasteful, wasteful!

Now fortunately there are other birds that are ground feeders, such as doves which are quite glad to take the waste. So nature has its balance.

This reminds me of the first time I went into a hardware store when I returned from Africa. When I left Canada as a missionary, a person could go to a hardware store and buy five screws or seven widgets. You could even buy one. But now a little clear plastic box glued to a two or three-coloured card, contains not one, but two, or six, or ten of whatever. If you need eleven, you have to buy twenty. If you need only seven, you have to buy twelve. And I'm convinced, in many cases, that the cost and quality of the packaging is higher than that of the product. We have to throw the most costly part away. Wasteful, wasteful, wasteful!

It's the same in our refrigerators. We buy more than we need, eat more than we should, and throw the rest into the garbage eventually. And people think it strange when some try not to wastefully dissipate their resources. Listen to 1 Peter 4:4:

"In regard to these, they think it strange that you do not run with them in the same flood of dissipation, speaking evil of you."

When I think of people in other parts of the world who would consider our throwaways riches, I wonder what God thinks of our waste?

Look at Proverbs 13:23:

"Much food is in the fallow ground of the poor, and for lack of justice there is waste."

When speaking of our way of doing things, we rationalize ourselves right out of common sense. It gets almost religious in its control. Paul commented on such self-imposed practices which are supposed to be good for us in Colossians 2:23:

"These things indeed have an appearance of wisdom in self-imposed religion, false humility, and neglect of the body, but are of no value against the indulgence of the flesh."

Of course, there's nothing sinful about having something valuable and having plenty to eat, but Solomon said in Proverbs 21:20:

"There is desirable treasure, and oil in the dwelling of the wise, but a foolish man squanders it."

It's the difference between folly and wisdom. One of the kings of the Old Testament got some very good advice from his mom that is found in Proverbs 31:9. These are the words of King Lemuel's mother:

"Open your mouth, judge righteously, and plead the cause of the poor and needy."

There is enough food in the world to feed the whole world. That's why I believe we have an obligation, especially if we call ourselves Christians, to do something about it. That's what righteousness is all about. Look at Matthew 25:34-36:

"Then the King will say to those on His right hand, 'Come, you blessed of My Father, inherit the kingdom prepared for you from the foundation of the world: for I was hungry and you gave Me food; I was thirsty and you gave Me drink; I was a stranger and you took Me in; I was naked and you clothed Me; I was sick and you visited Me; I was in prison and you came to Me.'"

Jesus explained very clearly that when we save and serve others, we are actually doing it to HIM. Let's stop wasting, and start sharing!

GLORIOUS IN MAJESTY

A blue jay may be just another screeching bird to you. But to me, it is another witness to the infinite and glorious majesty of the God of creation. Grass growing on a front lawn may just be another job to do; but to me, it's God revealed in nature. The change of seasons may just be an irksome necessity for different clothes to you; but to me, it is another indication of the infinite variety and resources of a God who loves me.

Just outside our front window is a rather vast lawn with two groves of birch trees, several maple trees, a few oak trees, a row of spruce down one side, and a row of pine down the other. It's nice and it's relaxing. Yet, it's not quite as beautiful as it can be unless there are birds. The other day, there were no birds, except in the distance. The reason? I had forgotten to fill our bird feeders. One of these bird feeders is directly in front of our living room window.

Since I like to get up and do something physical in between the writing of each commentary, I went out to the barn and got some grain to put into the bird feeders. The effect was almost immediate. When I sat down to write my next commentary, a beautiful blue jay had already arrived and was screeching out the news to one and all. Then all kinds of birds started to arrive.

It was a bit like a pastor, looking at all the birds in the distance and wondering why they aren't coming to roost in his pews. But as soon as he starts feeding them the riches of God's Word, they arrive in droves. Nothing better than a steady, well-balanced diet of the Word of God to fill the pews.

Let's go back to the blue jay on the bird feeder. I looked at it closely. None of the new car manufacturers have been able to duplicate the beauty and almost metallic quality of the blue on both the tail and the wings of a blue jay. I marvelled at the perfect fit of feather to feather, and the precision of movement of each little body feather as it slides to accommodate the movement of its head, neck and body. Then, as I looked at the black square framing its cosy blue collar around the neck and up to its crown, I wondered at the perfection of colour and movement in this beautiful symbol of my favourite baseball team. (I'm loyal, even when they lose!)

Then a male cardinal, gloriously red with his black bib, nervously pecked about as he had his meal. Then I saw a variety of sparrows with their different markings, and the finches dancing in the air around their special feeder. Once again, I was in awe of the God who made it all.

How can anyone not believe in God? And how can anyone think that God does not love His creation, and mankind in particular? He has given us everything to enjoy in abundance beyond our capacity to appreciate. He could have given us a bread and water diet of things to barely sustain us in life but, instead, He overflows us with good things. Look at what Paul says in Romans 8:32:

"He who did not spare His own Son, but delivered Him up for us all, how shall He not with Him also freely give us all things?"

King David also had a sense of the majestic and marvellous qualities of God revealed in what God has given us. Look at 1 Chronicles 29:11:

"Yours, O Lord, is the greatness, the power and the glory, the victory and the majesty; for all that is in heaven and in earth is Yours; Yours is the kingdom, O Lord, and You are exalted as head over all."

When I sit quietly in a church, I have that same sense of God's glory and power. Psalm 96:6 expresses it well for me:

"Honour and majesty are before Him; strength and beauty are in His sanctuary."

Yes, God has given us the greatest gift we could ever have, in the person and accomplished work of Jesus Christ. But with Him, He has given us all He has created and all that He Himself is. In Psalm 145:5, we read:

"I will meditate on the glorious splendour of Your majesty, and on Your wondrous works."

It's good to just sit down quietly and observe and think about all the good things God has given us. Sometime today, meditate on what the Lord really means to you.

PATIENCE - THE PERFECT WORK

I observed my chickens, and learned another lesson a while ago. I don't know if you have ever taken the time to watch a chicken. From the time she jumps up into a nest with the intention of laying an egg, right through until the time she lays the egg and jumps down from the nest with a happy grin on her beak, she rejoices loudly that nature has taken its course perfectly once again. She's the perfect picture of patience. And I must admit, it took a bit of patience to out-wait the egg!

It happens in the chicken coop all the time. A chicken gets an inner urge to get off by herself to produce an egg. I watched one of my old experienced girls hop up into a nest and shuffle around a bit (somewhat like a dog does before it lies down). Then this old hen nestled down, and simply waited. The picture of perfect patience.

She didn't make any fuss nor did she cackle or crow. She didn't grunt or groan, trying to force the process of nature. She just patiently waited for nature to take its course. Eventually, she raised herself a bit and, voila, a beautiful, perfect extra-large egg. The perfect picture of the rewards of patience.

Then the crowing began. She jumped out of the nest, strutted around cackling and crowing and rejoicing in the success of her newest project. The rest of the chickens joined in the general rejoicing and everyone lived happily ever after.... Well, not quite!

The human family hasn't lived happily ever after either. Human nature is not as patient as the rest of God's creation. Impatience has been the cause of many heartaches and problems in the human family. You can probably recall some uncomfortable incident in your own experience which was caused by impatience.

Yes, patience is a Christian virtue that most Christians don't practice too well. The Apostle Paul told a young preacher in 1 Timothy 6:11:

"But you, O man of God... pursue righteousness, godliness, faith, love, patience, gentleness."

Most of us get impatient. This is especially true when things are not going the way we had hoped, and our dreams and plans seem too far down the road. We try to force the issue. You can't force an apple tree to bear fruit in early spring. You can't force a chicken to lay a dozen eggs a day. Nature must take its course. And so it is with the plan and activity of God in our lives. We need patience, even in our own spiritual growth. Look at Luke 8:15:

"But the ones that fell on the good ground are those who, having heard the Word with a noble and good heart, keep it and bear fruit

with patience."

Impatience seizes us when we find ourselves in problems, particularly not of our own making. We want out of this problem, and we want out NOW. It seems our faith is severely tested at moments like this. But look at James 1:2-4:

"My brethren, count it all joy when you fall into various trials, knowing that the testing of your faith produces patience. But let patience have its perfect work, that you may be perfect and complete, lacking nothing."

As hard as it may seem in the middle of a great difficulty, that is the crucible God uses to bring us to perfection. Let patience have her perfect work! Allow God to bring you through victoriously. We have some pretty good examples of patient endurance, and Job is not the only one! Look at James 5:10:

"My brethren, take the prophets, who spoke in the name of the Lord, as an example of suffering and patience."

I think of Jeremiah, the prophet, who took a stand for justice and righteousness. Jeremiah faithfully spoke what God told him. He was treated with all kinds of abuse and indignity, and he never lived to see even one of his prophecies fulfilled. Yet, today, we can look back and see that his prophecies came true to the letter. And all the while, he patiently insisted that God's Word to him was true.

Take this lesson from the prophets — and from my chickens — because when patience has her perfect work, you will have something worth crowing about!

Chapter 9

Chicken, Goats, and One or Two Other Things...

PERVERTED VALUES

When I hear of a drowning, I am horrified. We have certainly had our share recently in Ontario, including a young acquaintance from a church near where we live. But when I heard of six people who drowned in an attempt to save the life of a chicken, I was doubly horrified. Can human life really be that cheap? In fact, what is the value of human life? Where should we draw the line when risking our necks?

It was a strange story in the *The Expositor* some time ago. The article certainly had an eye-catching title: "Six Drown While Trying To Save Chicken."

It appears that in an obscure village in a third-world country, a chicken had fallen into a well. The first person to attempt saving the chicken fell into the well and drowned. Next a 14 and 16-year-old made the attempt. They, too, drowned. Three more attempts were made, drowning all three people. When they finally retrieved the bodies from the well, they also brought the chicken out, alive and well!

Now, I have a few chickens of my own, and I would do anything reasonable to keep them from dying an unnatural death. I might even have tried to retrieve one from a well. But after two or three or four had died in the same attempt, I think I would have examined my value system. Is a chicken worth the lives of five or six people? Of course not. A chicken is worth a few eggs and finally, a meal.

It does beg the question: Why would so many people risk — in fact, lose their lives — to save one chicken? I doubt that it laid golden eggs, and even if it was a prize chicken, its value could hardly equal six human lives.

I don't know many good reasons for me to sacrifice my life. I would risk my life for a member of my own family, but I'm certain I wouldn't risk it for a chicken!

There are very few things for which I would risk my life, and financial gain is not one of them. Money is not much more than vapour in any case. Jesus put it in perspective when He said in Matthew 16:26:

"For what is a man profited if he gains the whole world, and loses his own soul? Or what will a man give in exchange for his soul?"

One life — one soul — is worth more than the whole world! Yet, in some parts of the world, life seems cheap and valueless. The reason for this is more related to one's soul than to life. There is an eternal value to the human soul. God loves you and values you very highly. Jesus said the whole world doesn't compare to the value of your soul. He also felt you were worth dying for. And that is love in its purest form. Look at John 15:13:

"Greater love has no one than this, than to lay down one's life for his friends."

To die trying to save a chicken by jumping into a well ends up being a horror story. To die to save another human being is a love story. Look at what used to be a familiar quotation in most Christian countries. John 3:16 says:

"For God so loved the world that He gave His only begotten Son, that whoever believes in Him should not perish but have everlasting life."

Although many people are not really familiar with this truth, it is the greatest love story ever known. That God would love you enough to jump into, not just a well, but this cesspool we call life and die for you and me is almost beyond comprehension. But God did it because He loves your eternal soul. He paid what would otherwise be your eternal penalty for sin, to provide you with eternal life.

You should be eternally grateful!

MORE FREEDOM THAN IS HEALTHY

Our goats are great, as long as we keep them under some semblance of control. When they get out of their yard where they have more than enough to eat and drink, they can cause a lot of damage, even to themselves. Well, they got out the other day and, for a while, they were out of our grace too. They are always taking liberties beyond reason. But, on the other hand, who says goats are reasonable? In fact, who says Christians are reasonable all the time?

My goats really 'get my goat' from time to time. Actually, they're not my goats. As I mentioned before, they really belong to my daughter Elaine. But we all share the responsibility of keeping them fed, watered, trimmed of their beautiful mohair, and kept generally happy and healthy. Like pastors!

But we do have restrictions on them. They have a good-sized, fenced-in yard with plenty of greens to eat and an old chicken house revised slightly to protect them from sun and rain. We are actually trying to keep them safe from several dangers. We don't want them to wander out onto the road, since goats and speeding cars don't mix too well. And we don't want them eating the leaves of our fruit trees, since we occasionally spray them with insecticides which might just give them an awful stomachache. We sure don't want them to eat from our vegetable gardens, since that might put us in the "dangerous" category, at least in attitude.

Regardless of our protective measures, these goats seem to want to get out and experience the world. We've patched the fence several times, and we suspect a few times that some mischievous child has simply unlatched the three catches on the door and let them out. The goats used to ram the door with their heads and make a break for freedom. Their theme seems to be, "Give me liberty, or give me a headache!"

Well, the other day they were out again. The latches were off the door. Someone was interfering with our security system. Mary and I went out to the garden when I got home, just to see how things were growing, and who do you think came bounding around the corner of the barn when they heard our voices? Right; two very pleased goats. When they hear our voices, they always come running now. I'm rather glad about that.

After we got them back into the security of their yard, we took a very close look to see what damage may have been done to our vegetable garden. Nothing for a change, except a bit of chewed up newspaper that I had been using to smother weeds. They had also uprooted, but not eaten, some of our petunias. They must have tasted these flowers, but not liked them too much.

Occasionally, a good Christian will get outside the fences the Lord has put around us for our safety. It may be a willful breaking out to have a taste of what's out there in the world. It may be the devil himself who enticed them with an open door. Even though King David stepped outside of God's boundaries when he had an immoral relationship with Bathsheba, he came running back in response to the voice of God. You see, it's a matter of the heart! David expressed himself in Psalm 42:1:

"As the deer pants for the water brooks, so pants my soul for You, O God."

Once people have tasted the good things of God, even when they step outside the boundaries by design or deception, God's voice will always call them to return. When the heart has been touched by God, the heart will respond to His call. He then will forgive and lovingly surround them with His protective boundaries. Look at Jeremiah 24:7:

"Then I will give them a heart to know Me, that I am the Lord; and they shall be My people, and I will be their God, for they shall return to Me with their whole heart."

Some folk feel they have offended God so badly that they go through all kinds of misery and self-inflicted punishments. They doubt that God will ever forgive them, since they can't seem to forgive themselves. Well, the good news is that God *will* forgive and restore. I give you the same message a prophet gave Israel in similar circumstances. Look at Joel 2:13:

"So rend your heart, and not your garments; return to the Lord your God, for He is gracious and merciful, slow to anger, and of great kindness; and He relents from doing harm."

So, hear the voice of God now and return. He loves you in spite of yourself, and He will forgive.

THE ONE LOST CHICK!

If you could have seen me the other day at dusk, you may have thought I was out of my mind. I was slowly stalking around my barn with a big fishnet in my hands. Now the river is 30 metres from my barn, and I don't grow fish in my barn. So, you may ask, "What in the world were you doing, waving a fishnet around at sunset? Is this some new religious ceremony you're starting?" No, but I will tell you what I was up to.

I have invested a lot in my 25 red chicks and, therefore, I want to protect my investment. That's why I lock them away in the barn at night. There are predators out there which would be glad for a free meal, and one of these little red pullets would make a handy meal for a fox or a racoon. So, I lock them up at night.

During the day, they have the freedom of the chicken yard, but it's restricted by a four-foot-high chicken wire fence. One of these young hens had decided to try her wings, and found that they worked quite well. She flew the coup! When I went to shut them away for the night, she was on the outside of the fence and at dusk was trying to find her way back in.

Well, I put the 24 away in the safety of the barn and then went to try to catch the little freedom-seeker who was now scared and trying desperately to run through the fence. She worked herself up into quite a state. When I approached to pick her up she ran around the barn a few times, and then I couldn't find her. She had fled under some bushes, or into a stand of trees, or maybe into one of my now lush gardens. I had one lost chick.

I know she wanted to be with the rest, but she couldn't find her way back in. Finally, she turned up again, desperately trying to get back. I finally caught her with a large fishnet. This was not the most comfortable experience I'm sure, but at least I got her in with her family again and she was safe for the night. In fact, she's probably safe for the rest of her life. But I'll tell you about that another time.

I felt sorry for this little lost hen and, besides, I had invested a lot in her. I bought her in the first place and had been feeding her for four months by now. I had cleaned house for her, and I didn't want to lose her at this stage.

I couldn't help thinking about that story found in Luke 15:4-7:

"What man of you, having a hundred sheep, if he loses one of them, does not leave the ninety-nine in the wilderness, and go after the one which is lost until he finds it? And when he has found it, he lays it on his shoulders, rejoicing. And when he comes home, he calls together his friends and neighbours, saying to them, 'Rejoice with me, for I have found my sheep which was lost!' I say to you that likewise there will be more joy in heaven over one sinner who repents than over ninety-nine just persons who need no repentance."

God has a great deal invested in you. He has given you the life, breath and health you have. He has given you the opportunity for freedom, joy, and the pursuit of happiness. He has given you food and drink and all you need, even though He does impose some boundaries. It's because He loves you. And besides all that, He has paid a great price for you. Listen to 1 Corinthians 6:19-20:

"Or do you not know that your body is the temple of the Holy Spirit who is in you, whom you have from God, and you are not your own? For you were bought at a price; therefore glorify God in your body and in your spirit, which are God's."

That price was the life of His own beloved Son, the Lord Jesus Christ. God has a lot invested in you, and just like I didn't want to lose my little red hen, God doesn't want to lose you either. And just as I didn't give up looking for (and finally catching) my little lost chick, God will not give up on you, even though you run off into the world for a while. There will come a time when you will want to be back in with God's family.

I'm inviting you to come NOW. It's dangerous outside His protection!

COOL AND REFRESHING

My new chickens were experiencing their first winter. It was a bit comical on one warm day when I let them out into the yard, even though there was snow on the ground. They rushed out, hit the snow and were back inside in a flash. Snow on bare feet, even chicken's feet, doesn't seem to be the cool thing to do. But when I come into the barn with snow on my boots, suddenly snow is all the rage and I have a dozen chickens pecking at my feet. Now there's a story here....

Even going out to the barn on winter days can be a cold business. You have to dress up warmly with hat, coat and boots. When the snow is crunching and squeaking under your feet, you know it's cold. Boots, fresh from the warmth of the house get covered with snow quickly and, at first, it melts. Then, before you get to the barn it freezes on your boots. You can pick up quite a load of snow before you step into the barn. It's still cold in there, until you get into the chicken coop area.

Chickens don't seem to like snow. On some warm days, even

though there's snow on the ground, I have offered them the freedom of the yard. When they see the door open, they immediately rush out. However, when they land on the snow, they come back in faster than they left. They don't like the stuff; that is, unless it's on my boots. I can stand there in the chicken coop, and a dozen chickens will gather around me pecking away at the snow on my boots.

It seems to be refreshing to them, and they like the sense of coolness in their beaks. They won't walk in the stuff, but they like to peck at it. I guess I'd rather not walk in snow in my bare feet but I don't mind ice in a drink, so why should I be surprised?

On a hot day, I relish a cool drink. When you're under the sun and the pressure is on, there's little that can measure up to a cold lemonade. I expect my chickens to give me 25 eggs a day. They're under their own pressure. A cool, refreshing interlude is wonderful, even if it is just snow on my boots.

Life for all of us could handle a time of refreshing; a cool drink; a pause of peace during the pressures. I think of the hard work and sweat of an old-fashioned harvesting. Snow would be a welcome substance right about then. Solomon thought so when he said in Proverbs 25:13:

"Like the cold of snow in time of harvest is a faithful messenger to those who send him, for he refreshes the soul of his masters."

But even better than snow when everything inside is all dried up, is a cold, refreshing drink of water. And sometimes, that's all that God requires of us: a cup of cold water to the thirsty. Jesus said in Mark 9:41:

"For whoever gives you a cup of water to drink in My name, because you belong to Christ, assuredly, I say to you, he will by no means lose his reward."

There were a few times in Africa when the most precious gift someone could have given me was a cup of water. Water is essential to life — whether it comes in the form of snow or plain water. It sustains our physical being, as well as the whole animal world, including my chickens. But there is another kind of water which does a deeper, and more effective good.

When Jesus met a Samaritan woman whom He discerned to be

dead and dried up in sin, he offered her something better than she was getting out of the nearby well. Listen to what Jesus said to her in John 4:10:

"Jesus answered and said to her, 'If you knew the gift of God, and who it is who says to you, Give Me a drink, you would have asked Him, and He would have given you living water.'"

Jesus went on to explain what he meant, and then in the final chapters of the Bible, He summarizes this great truth in Revelation 21:6:

"...It is done! I am the Alpha and the Omega, the Beginning and the End. I will give of the fountain of the water of life freely to him who thirsts."

Have you ever had this refreshing water of life?

SUCH BEAUTIFUL FLEECE!

Not everything and everybody is what they appear to be. Take my barnyard, for instance. It's not hard to tell a chicken from a duck, but I'm almost certain I could show you one animal that is very difficult to distinguish. It's especially true with people. Will the real Christian please stand up? Only the one under the fleece (and God, of course) really knows for sure....

We have two lovely animals which look for all the world like sheep. In fact, almost everyone who has been to our place and was not warned in advance have exclaimed something like, "Oh! You've got some sheep!"

They even sound like sheep. To almost everyone's surprise, they are goats. With some people, it even takes a little bit of doing to convince them that indeed they are goats. But they are a very special kind of breed: Angora goats, from which mohair is taken.

Their hair is so fine that a strand of it almost floats through the air. It is beautifully white and, in fact, soft and very cuddly. I've been told that it has to be mixed with wool from a sheep, or some other stronger fibre, in order to hold up its shape. Some new friends of ours, Ron and Nancy, are helping us turn it from simple fleece, into beautiful, workable skeins of mohair, dyed in several attractive colours. You'll see me yet in a sweater which Mary will knit for me. I'm looking forward to the day.

But there are a few things that come to mind when I think of these goats and their hair. First of all, they look like sheep, but they're goats. Secondly, their hair is beautiful and comfortable at first. Yet, as I mentioned before, anything made from mohair alone begins to sag and lose its shape, unless it has another strengthening fibre woven with it.

There are times when it is very difficult to see the difference between sheep and goats. There are times when it is very difficult to assess when a person is truly a Christian, or whether they are glib and well-disguised imitations. For this reason, none of us should pronounce judgment on another's spiritual status. God alone is the judge. He made that clear when, through the prophet, he said in Ezekiel 34:17:

"And as for you, O My flock, thus says the Lord God: 'Behold, I shall judge between sheep and sheep, between rams and goats.'"

We often think we know about someone's spiritual depth, strength or calibre. But only God knows!

Our judgment is often based on what we see; on how a person appears according to our perceptions of truth and error. That outward appearance can seem tremendously attractive and comfortable at first glance. But, given time, it may begin to sag and lose its initial beauty.

You can't imitate the Christian life forever. You can't mix a bit of faith with a bit of the world. Eventually a choice must be made. There's an interesting law found in Deuteronomy 22:11:

"You shall not wear a garment of different sorts, such as wool and linen mixed together."

I personally don't understand the reason for that law, but it is certainly an apt illustration of the need for clear decisions. Either you wear one or the other. Either you choose Christ and his pure robe of righteousness, or you reject him. We read in 1 Kings 18:21:

"And Elijah came to all the people, and said, 'How long will you falter between two opinions? If the Lord is God, follow Him; but if Baal, then follow him.' But the people answered him not a word."

Living like a goat in the guise of a sheep will end in disaster. Mixing the principles of the world with Christian convictions doesn't work. But no matter how much you've been like a dirty old goat, God is both forgiving and reasonable. Listen to this invitation from God, found in Isaiah 1:18:

"'Come now, and let us reason together,' says the Lord, 'Though your sins are like scarlet, they shall be as white as snow; though they are red like crimson, they shall be as wool.'"

You don't have to live a scrambled, mixed-up life. You can come dirty, and become clean. The secret is simply to COME!

Remember, it is Jesus who said, *"Come to Me, all you who labour and are heavy laden..."* (Matthew 11:28). So, why not come clean!

FEATHERS

One thing is certain, when you have a barn full of chickens, you also have feathers all over the place, especially at moulting time. When chickens are moulting, their egg production goes down. But when the moult is complete, production takes an up-swing, and the chickens certainly look much better. It's all controlled by something built right into their nature. If only we could change the nature of the beast, perhaps they'd act better in every way. Sounds a little like some people to me, in a way.

Just before a new season of laying eggs, chickens go through what is called a moult. My newest batch of Shaver Cross, which are a sub-breed of Rhode Island Red, have just now come to the point of laying. They've lost a whole mess of feathers, and have grown even more beautiful just as they are becoming productive.

I couldn't help but think of a woman who was once so self-centred and full of pride that she actually repulsed people. She was unproductive in everything but words and showiness. Then she... well... had a moult. Something happened that replaced the garishness with true joy and the ashes for real beauty — although it didn't have so much to do with the "outside," as with the "inside." Here's a poem I wrote about her, entitled "FEATHERS."

> I once saw a woman, so full of herself,
> That everything bought was from off the top shelf.
> She showed off and simpered and boasted to wear,
> The best clothes in the town, and with gold in her hair.

All covered in feathers, in bows and in lace,
She pretended to fame and to fortune and grace.
Her walk was determined, she projected great power,
Yet hid behind curls and makeup, a glower.

When seen from a distance, she was fancy with lace,
But when you got close, the look on her face
Would melt all the diamonds she wore with such pride,
And her heart had a hatred her eyes could not hide.

But then she met Jesus. What a difference it caused,
Now before dressing she thought, and she paused.
And her fine-feathered fancy stuff faded away.
Her face now took on beauty, in a placid sweet way.

I dare say she's much happier now than before,
And life in itself is much less of a chore.
Her heart has been changed by the power of love,
And she's clothed now in feathers much more like a dove.

I cannot help but think of the person whose life is hid with God in Christ. It's much like what the psalmist David described Israel as being when her trust was in the Lord. It's in Psalm 68:13:

"Though you lie down among the sheepfolds, yet you will be like the wings of a dove covered with silver, and her feathers with yellow gold."

And Psalm 91:4 states:

"He [God] shall cover you with His feathers, and under His wings you shall take refuge, His truth shall be your shield and buckler."

You wear your feathers better when you are under God's care and protection, and walking in His love. You can say with the great prophet Isaiah in chapter 61:10:

"I will greatly rejoice in the Lord, my soul shall be joyful in my God; for He has clothed me with the garments of salvation, He has covered me with the robe of righteousness, as a bridegroom decks himself with ornaments, and as a bride adorns herself with her jewels."

There is certainly nothing wrong with being well-dressed, and even expensively dressed, but when all it covers is a heavy and hateful heart, that's all it is: a covering.

But when the heart is in right relationship with God, the very glory and presence of Jesus — the Light of our lives — will only enhance whatever we put on the outside, whether it's rags or riches. Look at 2 Corinthians 4:6:

"For it is God who commanded light to shine out of darkness, who has shone in our hearts to give the light of the knowledge of the glory of God in the face of Jesus Christ."

Not only will your appearance change with obvious joy, peace and happiness, you will become productive.

Many Christians need to go through a moult. They need to have a change within, grow a new and better set of feathers, and become more productive for God.

But if it's just feathers you're interested in, come over to my barn — I've got a whole mess of them to give away. And, by the way, mess is the operative word. I could fill your trunk with them... and other things.

Take off the "gaudiness" and put on "godliness!"

OUR GOATS ARE "BONEHEADS"

How can nice people be so nasty? Why is it that some people have an impeccable public image, but their own families bear the brunt of their nastiness in the privacy of their own homes? We've got a couple of goats which illustrate this behaviour almost perfectly. When we are around them they are very cute, friendly, and even a bit nervous. But when they are alone, they can get really nasty with each other. Well, goats I think I can understand, but people? Even Christians? Let's look for the reason.

As I've mentioned before, my wife and daughter have two Angora goats. This is a special breed that produces mohair which many ladies love to have on the collars of their winter coats. It's both soft and warm. It makes beautiful wool.

What strikes me as strange is that such soft and warm wool can grow on such hard and ornery animals. They eat hay and love it, but they drag it out of the manger, trample it underfoot, then refuse to eat it. There are three doors in their pen in the barn. One of these doors leads into the rest of the barn which I use as a workshop.

These goats must have thick bones in their heads, because they seem to love butting each other in the head. They stand on their back legs facing each other, then come down together and butt their heads together with a meaty-sounding whack. I don't mind when they take it out on each other, but they've decided the doors are fair game as well. As a result of these warm and cute little boneheads, I have had to repair the main door to my workshop several times. They get loose into the rest of the barn, go up the stairs to my study loft I'm just finishing off, and leave their... well... let's call it "spoor" all over the place. How can an animal that appears to be so nice, have such an aggressive and nasty attitude?

I guess it's not too different from some people you and I have both met. They put on a very acceptable act for the public, but in their own homes they take on quite a different character. They feel their family can be the butt of their ill-tempered selves, but in public it's a different story. The reputation outside the home is impeccably respectable, but the immediate family knows a different side. I once knew a family like this and used to wonder why, even in public, their two children would duck or flinch if their dad made any kind of sudden movement. It all came out eventually. He was an ornery old goat, and was very abusive with the ones you would think he would love the most.

How do you suppose this can happen? Answer: It's a matter of the heart. Even some who call themselves Christians have that very peculiar heart disease. The Bible tells us about this in Jeremiah 17:9:

"The heart is deceitful above all things, and desperately wicked; who can know it?"

But aren't Christians supposed to have changed hearts? Don't we hear and teach, as it says in Ezekiel 36:26 that God...

"...will give you a new heart and put a new spirit within you; I will take the heart of stone out of your flesh and give you a heart of flesh?"

Then, where's the problem? The answer to that is found in Matthew 13:19:

"When anyone hears the word of the kingdom, and does not understand it, then the wicked one comes and snatches away what was sown in his heart. This is he who received seed by the wayside."

Hearing and even acknowledging the heart-changing Gospel of Jesus Christ is not quite enough. Unless God's Word takes permanent root in the heart, there is little real change, even though the outward appearance may change for a while.

Christians have traditionally used the expression, "Giving your heart to Jesus." That's more than just words. There is a very deep meaning to that expression, and it has everything to do with actually submitting your heart — the seat of your emotions — for God to control. James 4:7 says:

"Therefore submit to God. Resist the devil and he will flee from you."

You see, the Gospel of Jesus Christ is not merely a matter of words; it's a matter of a heart truly submitted to God and His ways. And His ways are written on the fleshly tables of the heart of anyone truly submitted to Him. And that's how you come to be a sheep in His flock.

Disguises won't work with God. In the end, God will separate the sheep from the goats. He knows the heart!

DOES GOD HAVE FAVOURITES?

As I have mentioned before, I did have a favourite hen. She was rather placid compared to other chickens. She was even a little overweight, like me. But she was my favourite. This hen was called a Plymouth (barred) Rock. She didn't produce as many eggs as other hens, nor did she put on any act of special niceness when I was around. Basically, she was my favourite because she pleased me. She never ran away from me squawking, but always came toward me very confidently. I like that!

Do you think God has any favourites?

My favourite hen was very prettily coloured. Her feathers seemed to line up in alternating bars of grey and white. She was a very heavy hen with lots of good muscle. She laid brown eggs which was good, because for some reason (which no one is quite able to explain) that's what most people prefer: brown eggs with strong shells. And although she laid fewer eggs by far than the white leghorns, I still favoured her.

Yet these qualities are not the real reason why I preferred this hen. My real reason was her nature. She was not like the high tension, nervous white Leghorns which scatter at any small or sudden movement or sound. And they don't necessarily scatter away from a perceived problem. In fact, they often flap and squawk right into the middle of whatever the commotion happens to be.

But this favourite hen of mine was a placid and quietly sedate little old lady. She might have been a bit nervous from time to time, especially when I took her into the studio with all the lights, and lots of people and cameras staring her in the beak. But she had a great nature, and brought a great deal of stability to the henhouse. She laid eggs (although less than many other chickens) and her doctrine was sound. She knew which came first: the chicken or the egg. She knew it was a chicken because, as she'd say in her Kentucky clucky, "God don't lay no eggs." God never makes a mistake. Yes, she was my favourite hen; not because of what she *did,* but because of what she *was!*

I have favourites in other things as well as chickens. People for instance. Some I like more than others. I like a chocolate milk shake much better than milk of magnesia. I like yellow beans more than green peppers. Certainly I have favourites! And these things are my favourites because they please me more than some other things. I have favourites! So what?

So does God! Now right away, I'm sure someone is saying God has no favourites. Well, I'm sorry, but He does! And His favourites are on the same basis. He favours those who please Him.

If you don't believe me, believe what His own Word says about it. Look at 1 Samuel 2:26:

"And the child Samuel grew in stature, and in favour both with the Lord and men."

Now why would God have favourites? I think it is made clear in Psalm 5:12:

"For You, O Lord, will bless the righteous; with favour You will surround him as with a shield."

Now before we go any further with this fact, I must make one thing abundantly clear. God loves all mankind equally, and with the same unchanging intensity. Just read what it says in Acts 10:34-35:

"Then Peter opened his mouth and said: 'In truth I perceive that God shows no partiality. But in every nation whoever fears Him and works righteousness is accepted by Him.'"

God's love is for all mankind, without exception, but He favours those who fear or reverence Him and live righteously. Look at Proverbs 12:2:

"A good man obtains favour from the Lord, but a man of wicked devices [intentions] He will condemn."

So, how can we become righteous enough to gain His favour? Good question! I'm glad you asked. Look at Romans 3:21-22:

"But now the righteousness of God apart from the law is revealed, being witnessed by the Law and the Prophets, even the righteousness of God, which is through faith in Jesus Christ to all and on all who believe. For there is no difference."

It's not how righteous you *act!* It's how righteous you *are* that counts with God. And simply believing makes you what you *are*. He loves you and gave His Son for you, because He's totally impartial. All men everywhere can come to God through Jesus Christ. When you do that, you take on the righteousness of Christ and God favours you. Not because of what you do, but because of what you become through believing in Jesus Christ.

Have you stepped into God's favour by accepting the righteousness of Jesus Christ?

THE SELF-MADE MAN?

"Man" (in reference to mankind) is such a creative creature! We've made it to the moon, and we send little cameras right inside the human body. We've made computers which can outstrip man in speed and accuracy. What wonders have been done, even by those who leave God out of their lives. Just think how powerful could be the creativity of a man or woman when completely surrendered to and empowered by God! Possible?

I get a real kick out of my daughter-in-law. She has a few forms of speech that are strange to me. The other day, I heard her say she was going to go to the kitchen and "make" an egg. I thought, Well, this must be an interesting procedure.

I followed her to her kitchen. She put an egg in boiling water and, well, boiled an egg. I said to her, "You said you were going to 'make' an egg. You're just boiling one that was already made. My chicken made that egg!" She laughed, and I laughed. I guess we both came to the conclusion that she can boil, scramble, poach, fry or just break an egg, but she can't make one.

Other people make claims of much the same kind, yet they are not merely forms of speech. They really mean it. One such saying is, "I'm a self-made man!" Yeah, sure, you just picked up a chunk of basic earth elements, and breathed into yourself the breath of life! I guess not!

What we are (and even what we do) has more to do with God than with us. Look at a very revealing verse in Isaiah 54:16:

"Behold, I have created the blacksmith who blows the coals in the fire, who brings forth an instrument for his work; and I have created the spoiler to destroy."

So many people I know discount God altogether. They say, "I don't even believe in God," or "Maybe there's some unknown power out there somewhere; but I'm on my own. If I'm going to get anywhere in life, I'm going to have to do it on my own. I'll work hard, study, pull the right strings, curry the favour of the right people and... voila, I'll make it happen! Yippee! I'm a self-made man (or woman)!"

And when that's all over, what then? I think "Saint Jimmy" had something to say about that in James 4:13-14:

"Come now, you who say, 'Today or tomorrow we will go to such and such a city, spend a year there, buy and sell, and make a profit'; whereas you do not know what will happen tomorrow. For what is your life? It is even a vapour that appears for a little time and then vanishes away."

If you want something created out of yourself that will last past the end of life, you've got to take a different route. This is the time when the final count on the number of toys will not matter. You have to acknowledge God as not just the Creator of life and the universe, but by what you *are* and *will be* throughout eternity. Ephesians 2:10 says:

"For we are His workmanship, created in Christ Jesus for good works, which God prepared beforehand that we should walk in them."

This applies to more than just blacksmiths. It applies to doctors, lawyers, premiers, presidents and preachers — the whole nine yards. And it's all through Jesus Christ, the Son of God; the image of the Creator who came down to mankind. Look at Colossians 1:15-16:

"He is the image of the invisible God, the firstborn over all creation. For by Him all things were created that are in heaven and that are on earth, visible and invisible, whether thrones or dominions or principalities or powers. All things were created through Him and for Him."

If you think you can live without God all your life... well, surprise, you can! But it's the "after-this-life" experience when all of that will come into focus.

If you don't live according to God's plan for you in this life, I can assure you, that's not the end of the matter. Listen to Hebrews 9:27:

"And as it is appointed for men to die once, but after this the judgment."

I'm not trying to scare you, and I'm not trying to tell you not to be energetic and take initiatives in life. I just want you to know the facts. And the facts are that God has more interest and involvement in your life than you can imagine. Why not make the best of it, by fitting in with His best plan for your creativity?

WHAT IS CROSSROADS FAMILY OF MINISTRIES?

In 1962, founder David Mainse began a weekly television ministry called Crossroads. In 1977, the television outreach expanded into the daily *100 Huntley Street* program. Today there are many additional facets of ministry at Crossroads.

■ Four regional Crossroads Ministry Centres – providing a 24-hour telephone prayer ministry across Canada.

■ Nine Circle Square Ranches, primarily a children's summer camping ministry.

■ Geoffrey R. Conway School of Broadcasting and Communications – focusing on the training of foreign students with a vision for starting TV ministries in their own countries.

■ The Family Centre – providing professional Christian counselling to those needing in-depth ministry.

■ Emergency Relief and Development Fund – helping people in crisis around the world in the Name of Jesus.

WAYS YOU CAN GET INVOLVED WITH THE MINISTRY OF CROSSROADS:

✓ Visit the Crossroads Centre and be a part of the "live" studio audience for a *100 Huntley Street* telecast.

✓ Become a volunteer telephone prayer partner at one of our Crossroads Ministry Centres.

✓ Become a supporting member at one of the following membership levels:

- Crossroads Foundation Member ($25 per month)
- Crossroads Builder Member ($50 per month)
- Crossroads Council Member ($83.50 per month = $1,000/year)

✓ Remember or honour someone special with a stone plaque on the Walk of Faith.

✓ Take advantage of Crossroads Financial Planning services for personal help with financial concerns such as preparing a Christian will.

HOW TO CONTACT US:

Call Crossroads at:
(905) 332-6400 ext. 5900 or 1-800-265-3100

or write to Crossroads,
P.O. Box 5100, Burlington, ON, L7R 4M2